JOBS, EARNINGS, AND EMPLOYMENT GROWTH POLICIES

JOBS, EARNINGS, AND EMPLOYMENT GROWTH POLICIES IN THE UNITED STATES

A Carolina Public Policy Conference Volume

edited by
John D. Kasarda

Kenan Professor
and Director,
Center for Competitiveness
and Employment Growth

The University of North Carolina
at Chapel Hill

Kluwer Academic Publishers
Boston   Dordrecht   London

Distributors for North America:
Kluwer Academic Publishers
101 Philip Drive
Assinippi Park
Norwell, Massachusetts 02061 USA

Distributors for all other countries:
Kluwer Academic Publishers Group
Distribution Centre
Post Office Box 322
3300 AH Dordrecht, THE NETHERLANDS

Library of Congress Cataloging-in-Publication Data

Jobs, earnings, and employment growth policies in the United States /
    edited by John D. Kasarda.
        p.   cm.
    "A Carolina Public Policy Conference volume."
    ISBN 0-7923-9105-5
    1. Manpower policy—United States.   2. Wages—United States.
I. Kasarda, John D.   II. Carolina Public Policy Conference.
HD5724.J665   1990
331.12′042′0973—dc20   90-33072
                                                                        CIP

Copyright © 1990 by Kluwer Academic Publishers

Printed in the United States of America

To

<small>Frank Hawkins Kenan</small>

who made the Kenan Institute of Private Enterprise possible

Contents

CONTRIBUTING AUTHORS

David L. Birch is Director of the Program on Job Creation and Corporate Change at Massachusetts Institute of Technology, and President of Cognetics, Inc., an economic consulting firm. A leading authority in the areas of employment, business growth, and economic change, Birch conducted landmark research in the late 1970s that first identified the critical role of innovation, particularly among small companies, in job creation, and has recently published the book, *Job Creation in America*. In 1980, the Small Business Administration named him "Researcher of the Year."

David E. Bloom is Professor of Economics at Columbia University, and previously taught at Carnegie-Mellon University and Harvard University. Bloom holds a Ph.D. from Princeton University. Known nationally for his distinguished research on demographic and labor force issues, Bloom has also published widely on the topics of employment and earnings in the United States.

Barry Bluestone is the Frank L. Boyden Professor of Political Economy at the University of Massachusetts/Boston and a Senior Associate at the university's John W. McCormack Institute of Public Affairs. In 1982, he wrote The Deindustrialization of America (Basic Books) with Bennett Harrision of Massachusetts Institute of Technology. *The Great U-Turn: Corporate Restructuring and the Polarizing of America* (Basic Books, 1988), also co-authored with Harrison, pursues the question of job quality and why the American worker is in trouble. Bluestone has served as executive adviser to the Governor's Commission on the Future of Mature Industries in Massachusetts and has worked closely with the Economic Development Department in the State of Michigan.

Robert E. Friedman, who is with CfED West in Hillsborough, California, is Chair of The Corporation for Enterprise Development, a Washington, DC-based not-for-profit economic development research, technical assistance, and demonstration organization. For over nine years, Friedman and CfED worked extensively with public and private policymakers in state and local governments, corporations, labor unions, and community groups to design and implement innovative and effective economic development strategies. Friedman is a graduate of Harvard College and Yale Law School.

Norman J. Glickman is Director of the Center for Urban Policy Research and Sate of New Jersey Professor of Urban Planning at Rutgers, The State University of New Jersey. He was recently Mike Hogg Professor of Urban Policy at the Lyndon Baines Johnson School of Public Affairs, the University of Texas at Austin. Professor Glickman, a specialist in urban and regional economics, has a Ph.D. in economics from the University of Pennsylvania. From 1970 until he joined the LBJ School faculty in 1983, he served on the faculty of the University of Pennsylvania as a Professor of Regional Science. Glickman serves as Chairman of the Austin Economic Development Commission. His most recent book, written with Douglas P. Woodward, is *The New Competitors: How Foreign Investors Are Changing the U.S. Economy* (Basic Books, 1989).

John D. Kasarda is Kenan Professor of Business Administration, Director of the Center for Competitiveness and Employment Growth, and a Fellow of the Carolina Population Center at the University of North Carolina at Chapel Hill. Dr. Kasarda is the author or co-author of six books and more than 50 scholarly articles on demographic and employment issues. He has testified a number of times before Congressional committees and has served as a consultant on urban economic development to the Carter and Reagan Administrations. On July 1, 1990, Dr. Kasarda becomes Director of the Frank Hawkins Kenan Institute of Private Enterprise at UNC-CH.

Marvin H. Kosters is a Resident Scholar and Director of Economic Policy Studies at the American Enterprise Institute, Washington, DC. The author of numerous books and scholarly articles on employment dynamics, his analyses of trends in jobs and wages have shown that the economic policies of the 1980s brought lower inflation and resumed growth in real incomes. Since receiving his degree in economics from the University of Chicago, Dr. Kosters has served as a senior economist at the White House, the Council of Economic Advisers, and the Cost of Living Council.

Thomas J. Plewes has been Associate Commissioner for Employment and Unemployment Statistics of the U.S. Bureau of Labor Statistics since January 1981. An employee of the Bureau of Labor Statistics since 1973, he has previously been a staff economist and Chief of the Data Services Group in the Office of Current Employment Analysis. Plewes is responsible for the bureau's programs of statistical data collection, analysis, and research in employment, unemployment, hours, and earnings. He has received the Department of Labor's Distinguished Career Service Award for his work in improving access to computer files for research and analytical purposes.

John Rees is Professor and Head of the Geography Department at the University of North Carolina at Greensboro. After receiving his Ph.D. from the London School of Economics, he taught at the University of Texas at Dallas (1975–83) and in the Maxwell School of Citizenship and Public Affairs at Syracuse University (1983–87). A well-published scholar in the fields of economic development, industrial location, and the impacts of public policy and technical change on regional growth in the United States, Dr. Rees has also conducted policy studies for the Joint Economic Committee of Congress, the General Accounting Office, the Office of Technology Assessment, and the Economic Development Administration.

James F. Smith is Professor of Finance in the Graduate School of Business Administration at the University of North Carolina in Chapel Hill where he is the author of the school's new bimonthly *UNC Business Forecast*, an analysis of the national and North Carolina economies. Dr. Smith is currently serving as vice president of the National Association of Business Economists, an organization of some 3,500 members. From September 1986 to September 1988 he was Director and Chief Economist of the Bureau of Business Research at the University of Texas at Austin.

Douglas P. Woodward is Research Economist for the Division of Research and Assistant Professor of Economics in the College of Business Administration at the University of South Carolina. He holds degrees in economics from the State University of New York, College of Purchase, New York University, and the University of Texas at Austin. He is the primary analyst for the *South Carolina Economic Indicators*. Dr. Woodward's research focuses on the regional impacts of foreign direct investment in the United States. He is co-author of *The New Competitors*.

ACKNOWLEDGMENTS

I would like to express my deep gratitude to Lynn Moody Igoe, manuscript editor at the Carolina Population Center, University of North Carolina at Chapel Hill, who skillfully copy-edited and managed the production of this volume.

I am also grateful to a number of other staff members of the Carolina Population Center. David Claris produced the figures on an Aldus PageMaker. Catheryn Brandon put electronic documents from various locations into workable formats. Lani Cartier and Nancy Kuzil entered documents for which there were no electronic files and Ms. Cartier proofread various stages of the book. Pat Wood, Laurie Ledbetter, Anny Thompson, and Chris Morris of the library staff worked tirelessly to verify bibliographic sources and members of the Humanities Reference Department at Davis Library were most helpful.

Special thanks go to Janet Jones, of the Department of Sociology, who assisted in word processing and coordinating activities.

Basic Books has graciously granted permission to reprint the figures in Chapter 4, previously used in Norman J. Glickman and Douglas P. Woodward's book *The New Competitors: How Foreign Investors Are Changing the U.S. Economy* (1989).

INTRODUCTION

John D. Kasarda

By all accounts, the United States has led the world in job creation. During the past 20 years, its economy added nearly 40 million jobs while the combined European Economic Community added none. Since 1983 alone, the U.S. generated more than 15 million jobs and its unemployment rate dropped from 7.5 percent to approximately 5 percent while the unemployment rate in much of western Europe climbed to double digits. Even Japan's job creation record pales in comparison to the United States', with its annual employment growth rate less than half that of the United States over the past 15 years (0.8 percent vs. 2 percent.)

Yet, as the U.S. economy has been churning out millions of jobs annually, conflicting views and heated debates have emerged regarding the quality of these new jobs and its implications for standards of living and U.S. economic competitiveness. Many argue that the "great American job machine" is a "mirage" or "grand illusion." Rather than adding productive, secure, well-paying jobs, most new employment, critics contend, consists of poverty level, dead-end, service-sector jobs that contribute little or nothing to the nation's productivity and international competitiveness. Much of the blame is placed on Reagan-Bush policies that critics say undermine labor unions, encourage wasteful corporate restructuring, foster exploitative labor practices, and reduce fiscal support for education and needed social services. The outcome, according to this view, is higher profits but lower wages, an erosion of the middle class, and the formation of an increasingly polarized nation composed of investment bankers and corporate lawyers at one end and hamburger flippers and car washers at the other.

That perspective has been vigorously contested by scholars and government officials more sympathetic to Reagan-Bush policies who marshall data and arguments that present a much more favorable portrayal of the quality of jobs being created, earnings distributions, and productivity growth. According to this group, increases in employment have actually been greater in occupations with higher average wages; there has been no surge in income inequality; corporate restruc-

1

turing has resulted in improved productivity in recent years, and greater use of nonunionized, contingent workers cuts labor costs and thereby strengthens the competitive position of U.S. businesses.

In this context of conflicting data, analyses, and interpretations, the Center for Competitiveness and Employment Growth of the Kenan Institute of Private Enterprise at the University of North Carolina at Chapel Hill assembled leading figures in the debate to articulate their positions and conduct open dialogue. Efforts were made to pair formal presentations and discussants to clarify issues and untangle misunderstandings. We also sought to move beyond the ''good jobs'' versus ''bad jobs'' debate by bringing in distinguished scholars and discussants to assess factors underlying the job creation process, including the sources of employment growth, characteristics of businesses creating the most new jobs, the relative importance of direct foreign investment, and the role of government in facilitating entrepreneurial success, quality job growth, and national economic revitalization.

The five chapters and associated commentaries which follow derive from this Carolina Public Policy Conference on Job Creation for the Nineties. They offer highly diverse and oftentimes provocative assessments of job trends in the United States, their causes and consequences, and policy prescriptions. Chapters 1 and 2, highlighting the quality of jobs debate, are by Barry Bluestone (University of Massachusetts, Boston) and Marvin Kosters (American Enterprise Institute), respectively. Bluestone's critical perspective is discussed by Thomas Plewes, Associate Commissioner of the U.S. Bureau of Labor Statistics, while Kosters' more favorable evaluation is commented upon by David Bloom of Columbia University.

Bluestone's principal position is that despite the prolific number of jobs generated in the U.S., real wages have stagnated and income inequality has risen markedly since 1973. He provides analyses indicating that wage stagnation and growing inequality have been invariant to upswings in the business cycle and demographic shifts in the labor force. Thus, he sees little prospect for improvement in these trends as a result of a continuation of the national economic recovery and eventual shift from the ''baby boom'' to the ''baby bust'' generation in the labor force. Drawing on his own research and that of others, Bluestone argues that deindustrialization, declining unionization, and the minimum wage freeze have combined to disadvantage the American worker. He also shows that industrial restructuring has increased the degree of wage dispersion by dramatically increasing the returns to higher education while reducing income returns to those who complete only a secondary school education or less. Bluestone's policy prescriptions lie in improving access of all segments of society to better education, maintaining our manufacturing job base, strengthening labor unions, and increasing the minimum wage.

Thomas Plewes, in commenting on Bluestone's chapter, concurs regarding the importance of education but offers alternative views to Bluestone's other positions. Plewes believes that increasing global competition since the early 1970s, especially in manufacturing, has required new strategies to reduce labor costs and increase work force flexibility (e.g., greater use of nonunionized and contingent workers); otherwise jobs would be lost entirely. He concludes with a number of caveats to Bluestone's policy recommendations concerning reindustrialization, reunionization, and minimum wage increases.

Marvin Kosters' working thesis is that the more market-oriented policies of the Reagan-Bush era have produced better economic performance and work force outcomes than those where government has interfered with the marketplace. He constructs a variety of alternative earnings measures to challenge the conclusion of Bluestone and others that workers' real earnings have been falling since the early 1970s and that incomes have become more polarized. Kosters illustrates the point that "facts" rarely speak for themselves by describing the intricacies of using different measures to produce different results and conclusions about how the work force is faring. For example, the striking difference in trends in average hourly *compensation* and average hourly *earnings* is explained when one recognizes that the latter excludes payments for such benefits as health insurance, social security, and retirement plans.

Assessing factors influencing stagnating real wages, Kosters considers the productivity slowdown in the 1970s as most significant. He also argues that the spreading distribution of family incomes since the early 1970s has resulted largely from rising numbers of households headed by single mothers and the simultaneous increase in the number of families with two or more adults in the work force.

Kosters closes his chapter with an effort to buttress his pro-market thesis by comparing trends in employment and earnings during the Carter-Mondale administration with those of the Reagan-Bush administration and by comparing the post-1980 jobs, earnings, and productivity experience of the United States with that of O.E.C.D. Europe where market intervention by governments is more extensive. These comparisons lead him to conclude that government policies that artificially prop up wage levels, redistribute income, and impede labor force adjustment have, in the net, negative consequences for workers and the economy.

David Bloom comments that Kosters' and Bluestone's chapters each reveal how analysts can conjure up evidence consistent with their ideological preconceptions. He chides Kosters for not living up to the analytical rigor that Kosters himself calls for in critiquing the work of others. Bloom also calls for research that moves beyond debates over measurement to broader issues such as considering the "ideal" distribution of jobs and incomes to which a nation should aim and the processes by which jobs and income distributions are created.

The second half of the conference resulting in Chapters 3, 4, and 5 in this volume takes us in that direction. Chapter 3 by David Birch (derived from his luncheon address) offers an overview of his research program at M.I.T. which seeks to understand the firm-level sources of employment growth and decline and how the welfare of individuals and communities relates to these dynamics. Linking records on 17 million individual businesses derived from the Dun and Bradstreet Market Identification Files, Birch has developed a 20-year history of each of these establishments which today employ about 95 percent of the private sector work force. This has enabled him to break down aggregate employment change in the United States into that caused by firm births, deaths, expansions and contractions, firm inmigration and outmigration and to determine the size, age, ownership, and other characteristics of businesses creating the most jobs.

Birch's results show that the corporate population is an enormously turbulent one, with 50 percent of the jobs created by individual business turning over every five years. There is also an immense amount of restructuring taking place in what he labels "the new economy." He finds that while the Fortune 500 companies have laid off more than 3 million American workers during the 1980s, 1.3 million new enterprises are starting each year, and a portion of them are growing very rapidly, more than replacing the job losses resulting from firms shrinking in size, moving employment off shore, or shutting down entirely.

Birch is probing the characteristics of these rapidly growing companies, the kinds of jobs they are creating, and whether these new jobs are better, worse, or simply different from the ones they are replacing. He is also concerned with the characteristics of particular communities that seem to spawn disproportionate numbers of rapid growth firms, including their locations and human capital resources. Finally, Birch is assessing how growing global economic interdependence is affecting U.S. companies and thereby shaping the life chances of individuals and communities associated with these companies.

Norman Glickman and Douglas Woodward (Chapter 4) focus on the receiving end of growing global economic interdependence in their assessment of the extent to which direct foreign investment in the United States is creating jobs and revitalizing the economy. They present rich information about who is investing in America, characteristics of the foreign firms acquiring U.S. businesses, how much of the American economy they own, what industries they are concentrated in, where they are located, and, most germane to this volume, how many jobs foreign investors are actually creating in the United States.

Their principal finding is that since foreigners typically purchase existing plants and businesses, they are creating relatively few jobs and simply transferring corporate ownership. Glickman and Woodward describe how, in many cases, leveraged buyouts, mergers, acquisitions, and corporate restructuring by foreign investors have resulted in marked declines in employment in U.S. facilities.

Although direct foreign investment grew by 17 percent a year through the 1980s, Glickman and Woodward show that foreign ownership of American companies is still relatively small with only 3.5 percent of U.S. workers and 8 percent of productive assets under foreign control. Of these U.S. workers controlled by foreigners in 1988, Great Britain led the way with 21.5 percent, followed by Canada (20.3 percent), West Germany (10.3 percent), Netherlands (8 percent), Japan (7.3 percent), and France (6.5 percent). Like American firms investing abroad, Glickman and Woodward find that most foreign investment is in manufacturing (32.5 percent). Whereas foreign ownership has been historically concentrated on the East Coast and South, the Midwest and West have attracted a good deal of investment from abroad during the past decade, especially from Asia. However, they show that the kinds of investments that create jobs—new plants and expansions of existing businesses—are still geographically concentrated in the South.

Glickman and Woodward see foreigners as here to stay and becoming a growing part of the U.S. economy if we don't deal more effectively with our trade and budget deficits and productivity problems. They close with a series of policy recommendations for the U.S. to restore competitiveness of its domestic industries, protect American communities and workers from plant closings and job displacement, and control the bidding war among states and localities anxious to attract foreign investment to bolster their employment and tax bases.

James Smith's commentary takes a far more sanguine view of direct foreign investment and free market processes than Glickman and Woodward. Consequently, he finds little merit in their policy prescriptions. Smith notes that prior to this century, the majority of U.S. job creation and industrial growth was funded by foreign investors and that today U.S. direct investment abroad far exceeds that of foreigners in the United States. He considers Glickman's and Woodward's recommendation to address problems of the U.S. economy as a throwback to the Carter-Mondale era that would be wasteful and counterproductive. Like the Bluestone-Kosters et al. debate in Chapters 1 and 2, Smith's discussion once again highlights the point that public policy, stripped to its basics, represents a choice among value alternatives.

Robert E. Friedman (Chapter 5) investigates job creation in light of three waves of modern state economic development, beginning in 1936 with the South's efforts to lure manufacturing plants from the North by offering low labor costs, cheap land, and limited government interference. The second wave, Friedman claims, began in New England in the 1970s where, in the midst of deindustrialization and worker displacement, those states discovered and fostered the growth of new, smaller businesses, primarily in the information and business service sectors. He then outlines features of the emerging third wave of economic development based on creativity, entrepreneurship, strategic financing, business networking, and renewed investment in human capital.

Friedman explains the Development Report Card for the States, a device designed by the Corporation for Enterprise Development and used as an index to measure the varied dimensions of economic health of states and their workers and citizens. The Report Card assesses and ranks states in four broad areas: economic performance, business vitality, capacity, and public policy.

In applying the Report Card to achievements of the second wave of economic development, Friedman finds serious problems: (1) piecemeal approaches to development, (2) lack of integration of social and economic policy, and (3) lack of accountability. When he looks at development associated with the third wave, Friedman targets five areas for programmatic emphasis: education, development finance, investment in the poor, business assistance, and entrepreneurial systems.

Friedman joins Bluestone, Kosters, and others in stressing the need for improvements in the American educational system to produce a work force with the appropriate level of skills. He suggests a change in private-sector investment activities for individuals and institutions as a way to bolster development finance, using the successful Michigan Strategic Fund as an example. His comments on disadvantaged persons stress the notion of investing in the poor rather than merely offering them welfare programs. Friedman also recommends a network approach to business assistance rather than the old one-to-one method and gives examples of successes in European networking to start new businesses, create jobs, and raise standards of living. In his closing discussion of entrepreneurial systems, which he sees as being the cornerstone of the third wave, Friedman stresses that entrepreneurship must apply not only to small firms in the private sector but also to large corporations, the non-profit sector, and government agencies.

John Rees's discussion of Friedman's chapter concludes this volume. Rees is wary of the political motivation underlying the indices selected by Friedman for his Report Card on the States as he is of efforts in general to measure state "business climate." Rees is, however, quite complimentary of Friedman's emphasizing the role of the entrepreneur and entrepreneurialism in job creation and economic development policies. He is less enthusiastic about Friedman's call for accountability and evaluation of new economic development policies, at least as presently conducted by most states. According to Rees, creativity, innovation, and long-run economic growth may be stifled if political evaluations only consider such short-term surrogates as the number of jobs created or matching funds obtained.

Taken together, the five chapters and discussions which follow enrich our understanding of recent developments in U.S. labor markets, document significant changes occurring in the broader economy, and exemplify the key issues and views shaping current policy debates on job growth, wages, and economic development strategies. They provide highly informative reading to all those concerned with the future of the American economy and the status of its work force.

1 THE GREAT U-TURN REVISITED: ECONOMIC RESTRUCTURING, JOBS, AND THE REDISTRIBUTION OF EARNINGS

Barry Bluestone

In December 1986, the Joint Economic Committee (JEC) of the U.S. Congress made public its commissioned report, "The Great American Jobs Machine" (Bluestone and Harrison, 1986). It was to become one of the committee's most controversial of the year. The "Jobs Machine" study concluded that during the 1980s the U.S. economy continued to churn out new jobs at about the same rapid pace as during the previous decade, but a majority of the jobs created after 1979 were of dubious quality as measured by the annual earnings they paid.The JEC report revealed that while more than 20 million additional jobs were generated in the United States between 1973 and 1984, nearly three out of five (58 percent) of the net new jobs created after 1979 paid $7,400 or less a year (in 1984 dollars). In contrast, fewer than one in five of the additional jobs generated between 1963 and 1979 had paid such low wages.[1]

These statistics did not come as a particular surprise to those who had been focusing their attention on the steadily declining number of high-wage manufacturing jobs or those who regularly counted the growing number of help wanted advertisements for low-wage jobs in the fast-food industry or for positions as building janitors, security guards, and nurse's aides. Nonetheless, the report provoked a spate of criticism.[2] Typical of popular reaction was that of then-Secretary of Labor, William E. Brock. In the *Washington Post*, Brock (1987) suggests that "new life has been injected into this 20th Century Flat Earth Society" comprised of believers in the "bad job myth." The American economy, he argues, is generating millions of new "good" jobs in high-paying fields such as transportation, public utilities, communications, finance, banking, insurance, and data processing. Indeed, he concludes, "In the five years of the recovery [1983–87], only one major segment of the job sector has declined: minimum-wage jobs have fallen 25 percent, while those jobs paying $10 an hour or more have increased by 50 percent."

Such conflicting views of the jobs data as represented by the JEC report and the highest senior official of the Labor Department whetted the appetite of a small cadre of social scientists. What followed was something of an academic battle royal. Today, after a great deal of statistical jousting, there is near unanimous agreement that wages have stagnated and earnings inequality has increased (for an excellent review of the statistical evidence, see Loveman and Tilly, 1988). But, in dozens of journal articles, monographs, and books, protagonists in the debate have moved beyond debating the wage trends themselves to skirmishes over the underlying causes of these labor market outcomes.

Drawing on the work of many of the participants in this debate, I review the evidence to date concerning employment and earnings patterns in the United States beginning in the early 1960s. In the next section of this chapter, I sketch out a set of fundamental changes that occurred in the composition of the labor force between 1963 and 1987. I then review the evidence on changing patterns in wage inequality according to a number of statistical measures. In the fourth section I describe the various hypotheses advanced to explain the changing pattern in wage growth and wage dispersion. Next I provide evidence for and against each of these hypotheses. Finally, I attempt a new synthesis of these theories and comment on possible implications.

The general findings of this chapter can be summarized as follows. First, there is now overwhelming evidence that real wages have stagnated, and wage inequality has increased at least since the early 1970s and has continued to do so right through the economic recovery of the 1980s. Second, wage stagnation and rising wage inequality is largely independent of the business cycle and has little to do with the entrance of the "baby boom" generation into the labor market. Third, changes in industrial structure and such concomitant institutional factors as the decline in unionization have contributed to the growth in inequality. And, finally, the changing industrial structure has increased the degree of wage dispersion in the United States by acutely increasing the relative returns to postsecondary education while reducing the returns to those who complete no more than the high school degree. Because little of the increase in earnings inequality is related to demographics or the business cycle, there is little chance that this trend will disappear simply as the result of a shift from the baby boom to the baby bust generation, or merely as a consequence of steady, but modest, growth in aggregate economic output. Improvements in educational access, attempts at maintaining manufacturing employment, and expanded unionization and minimum wage protection may be the only workable means to reverse the trend toward "polarization" in the U.S. labor market.

CHANGING AMERICAN EMPLOYMENT PATTERNS

As background to an exploration of recent wage trends, it is useful to begin with some baseline data concerning changes in the characteristics of the American work force (see Table 1.1). Several major trends are obvious. Women are on the verge of becoming virtually half of the employed labor force, having increased their labor force participation substantially since the early 1960s. There has also been an increase in the nonwhite share of the labor force, but over the nearly 25-year period depicted in Table 1.1, the minority share has grown by less than 2.5 percentage points. The flow of the baby boom bulge through the labor force is easily detected in the data. From 1963 to 1973, workers aged 16–24 expanded their share of total employment by 5.7 percentage points before the baby bust generation entered the labor market. Then the pattern reversed, especially after 1979. By 1987, the youngest age cohort actually comprised a smaller share of the total work force than in 1963.

At the other end of the age spectrum, older workers—those 55 and above—have become an ever smaller share of the work force, falling from more than a sixth to only an eighth of the total. Essentially, then, during the 1980s the work force became increasingly "prime age" and more labor market experienced. In 1963, 61.4 percent of the total work force was aged 25–54; by 1987, the comparable figure was 66.7 percent.

The labor force has also become better educated, at least as measured by years of school completed. As late as 1963, nearly 45 percent of the total work force

Table 1.1   The Changing Nature of American Employment, 1963–87 (in percentages)

Worker Characteristics	1963	1973	1979	1987
Female	38.2	41.9	44.8	47.0
Nonwhite	11.3	11.7	12.0	13.7
Age				
16–24	21.3	27.0	26.0	20.8
25–34	20.1	23.2	26.9	29.0
35–54	41.3	34.5	33.2	37.7
55+	17.3	15.3	13.9	12.6
Education				
Less than high school diploma	44.7	31.3	24.3	18.3
High school graduate	33.8	38.8	39.8	40.8
Some college	11.2	15.4	18.5	21.4
College degree or more	10.3	14.5	17.4	19.5
Industry				
Manufacturing	25.3	24.8	23.0	19.1
Services & trade	42.7	52.5	55.1	60.1
Year-Round Full-Time	52.4	56.2	55.8	60.4

Source: Special tabulations from the Current Population Survey Annual Demographic Files, March 1964–March 1988. The percentages refer to all workers on the March files with some earnings in the previous calendar year.

had not completed high school. Fewer than 25 years later, only 18 percent had so little formal education. Meanwhile, the college trained share of the work force—those with at least some postsecondary schooling—has practically doubled from 21.5 to 40.9 percent. The percentage with college degrees or schooling beyond the bachelor's degree has nearly doubled as well. While American workers were becoming more schooled and more job experienced, the underlying structure of the economy was simultaneously shifting from a manufacturing base to one increasingly dominated by "postindustrial" services. Manufacturing employment fell from better than a fourth of the work force to less than a fifth between 1963 and 1987. Services and trade employment rose accordingly from about two-fifths of total employment to more than three-fifths.

Finally, despite the growth in part-time employment, the percentage of the work force working year-round, full-time (YRFT)—50 or more weeks a year and usually 35 hours or more per week—actually expanded 8 percentage points in 24 years.[3] This trend was almost exclusively because of the increase in women's year-round, full-time work.

In a nutshell, the work force has become significantly more schooled, more prime age, and more fully attached to the labor market. On the surface, all of these factors should be leading to higher annual earnings and less low-wage employment. That an ever larger share of the labor force is comprised of women who have traditionally been paid less than men might very well lead average wages in the opposite direction. But, as I demonstrate, the U.S. employment and earnings story is far more complicated than these simple demographic trends suggest.

THE TREND IN REAL WAGES AND WAGE DISPERSION

The postwar history of real wages in the United States is a fascinating one in itself. As Figure 1.1 indicates, real average weekly earnings of the total work force rose steadily from the end of World War II until 1973. Since then, weekly earnings have generally moved downward. This trend holds true regardless of the price deflator used to translate nominal wages into real earnings. Overall, average weekly earnings in 1987 were 16 percent below the level prevailing in the early 1970s if one relies on the consumer price index (CPI-U-X1); they are still 9 percent lower with the more conservative personal consumption expenditures deflator (PCE). Murphy and Welch (1988, Table 1) find precisely the same U-turn pattern in hourly, weekly, and full-time annual wages for the group traditionally most favored in the labor force, white men. As I show later, this U-turn in real average wages is the first in a pattern that repeats itself with great regularity.[4]

Aggregate Measures of Wage Dispersion

While there has been little dispute as to the general trend in average wages,[5] the question of a trend in the *distribution* or dispersion of earnings is a different matter.

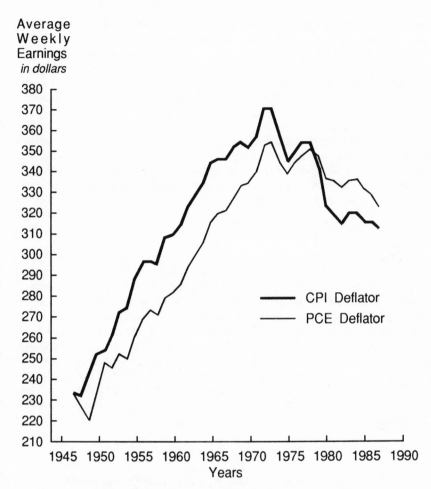

Source: Council of Economic Advisers, *Economic Report of the President,*
          February 1988

Figure 1.1   Real Average Weekly Earnings, 1947–87   (1987 Dollars)

Here, the issue of increasing inequality beginning in the early 1970s has been
keenly debated.

Research started in the late 1970s began to uncover a pattern of rising inequality in wage income as measured by traditional measures such as the variance in
the log of earnings (VARLNWAGE) and the Gini coefficient. Working from a
data source which would become the standard for all such work—the Annual

Demographic File of the *Current Population Survey*, Henle and Ryscavage (1980) found evidence of increasing inequality among male earners beginning in 1966 and then stabilizing from 1974 to the end of their time series in 1977. They found no such pattern for women. Dooley and Gottschalk (1984) confirmed these findings and further found the increase in male earnings inequality could not be explained away by changes in education, work experience, unemployment, or the age of the labor force.

In more recent work along the same lines, Gary Burtless of the Brookings Institution has used various distribution measures to investigate longer term trends in inequality. Using Bureau of the Census P-60 Reports, Burtless finds secularly growing Gini coefficients for men and women beginning after World War II, indicating slow but steady increases in earnings inequality. For men, the Gini rises from .265 in 1947 to .429 in 1986; for women the comparable coefficients are .386 and .460, but with virtually all of the growth preceding the 1970s. Relative to other distributions (e.g. family income), these Ginis reflect very substantial inequality growth.[6]

All of these previous studies were focused on men and women separately. However, when Harrison, Tilly, and Bluestone (1986) and then Tilly, Bluestone, and Harrison (1987a) combined men and women into a single series in an attempt to proxy the structure of the full underlying jobs distribution, they found a pattern not unlike that for average wages. Instead of secularly rising earnings inequality, they found the first of what would turn out to be a whole series of U-turns in wage dispersion. Adopting VARLNWAGE as the measure of inequality and including all workers with some earnings in a given year, they found that wage inequality actually declined sharply from 1963 through 1978 before abruptly reversing course. After 1978, earnings inequality increased as quickly as it had declined so that by 1987 it had returned to a level higher than that 20 years earlier.[7] (See Figure 1.2.)

Wage Shares over Time

An alternative approach to studying wage patterns over time relies on an extension of the original Bluestone and Harrison JEC analysis of wage shares. The trend in real weekly earnings provides insight into the average value of jobs in the economy. The trend in wage dispersion isolates the pure distribution effect. The Bluestone and Harrison approach, later adopted by Kosters and Ross (1987, 1988) and the U.S. Senate Budget Committee (1988), combines both measures into one. Real wage shares account simultaneously for changes in the average wage and in the wage distribution. They measure the proportion of the work force falling within various wage strata in *real* dollar terms at different points in time.

The original JEC study of wage shares had a number of methodological deficiencies. Janet Norwood, Commissioner of the Bureau of Labor Statistics (1987), suggests, for example, that to prove a secular pattern in wage shares adequately, one must estimate and decycle a complete time series rather than choose particular

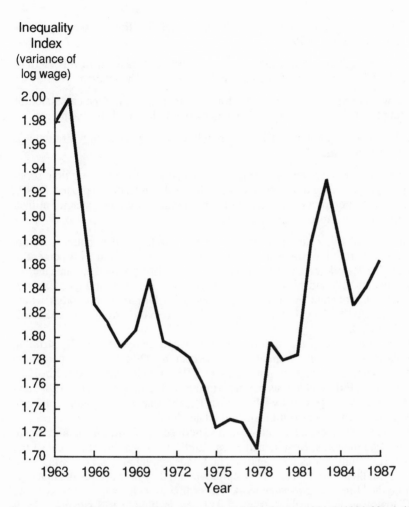

Source: Annual Demographic Files, *Current Population Surveys,* March 1964–March 1988

Figure 1.2   Inequality in Annual Wages and Salaries, 1963–87

years as was done in the initial JEC research. Moreover, the original analysis had included part-time and part-year workers in the sample as well as year-round, full-time workers. This, she argues, confounded any annual earnings results by confusing possible changes in hours worked with changes in real wage rates.

To accommodate both criticisms, Bluestone and Harrison (1988) reorganized and expanded the original JEC analysis using the following methodology:

1. The median annual earnings for all year-round, full-time workers age 16 or over was calculated for 1973.[8]

2. A low-wage cutoff was arbitrarily assigned at 50 percent of this median. Similarly, a high-wage cutoff was set at 200 percent of the median.

3. Low and high real wage cutoffs for 1963 to 1987 were then calculated by adjusting the 1973 cutoffs to the Consumer Price Index (CPI) for each year.[9]

4. The proportion of all YRFT workers falling into each earnings stratum was tallied for each year.

5. Finally, to remove any business cycle component, the resulting time series was decycled according to six different variables: real gross national product (GNP), log GNP, the unemployment rate, log unemployment rate, the capacity utilization rate, and log capacity utilization.[10]

The result of this estimation procedure was another U-turn pattern. Before decycling, the raw low-wage share shows a sharp decline from 21.4 percent of the total YRFT work force in 1963 to 12.5 percent in 1970; it fluctuates in a narrow band between 12.5 and 13.9 percent between 1970 and 1979 and then expands rapidly to 16.2 percent by 1987. (See Figure 1.3.) Moreover, no matter which variable is used to decycle the trend, the U-turn remains strongly in evidence. (See Figure 1.4.)

Trends in the size of the middle- and high-wage shares are equally striking, the middle stratum falling from nearly 81 percent in 1970 to only 75.3 percent in 1987. In contrast, the high-stratum share of YRFT employment peaked in 1973 at 9.1 percent, fell to as low as 6.5 percent during the recession year 1981, and then recovered to 8.5 percent by 1987. Taken together, the three trajectories indicate an increase in wage polarization since the late 1970s.

There is now evidence that this U-turn pattern survives after using alternative deflators and medians. Kosters and Ross (1988), who were most critical of the original JEC study, focus their analysis on trends among all workers. But, when they do turn their attention to YRFT employment, they produce results that corroborate the U-turn in low-wage work. According to their own calculations, the YRFT low-wage share declines from 17.2 percent in 1967 to 10.1 percent in 1979 and then rises nearly steadily to 13.8 percent by 1985 (see their Table 14). In fact, the Kosters-Ross results actually indicate a much steeper proportional rise in the low-wage share between 1979 and 1985 than do our own calculations. For a critical review of Kosters and Ross' research that demonstrates consistency between their estimates and those of Bluestone and Harrison, see Mishel (1988).

Further analysis of the CPS survey data reveals that the U-turn in the low-wage employment trend and the drift toward polarization are found among many demographic groups, across all four census regions, and within manufacturing and service industries. Table 1.2 provides data for selected years on the low-wage share of employment among YRFT workers. Note that for nearly every group, there is a sharp decline in the low-wage proportion between 1963 and 1973,

Percentage

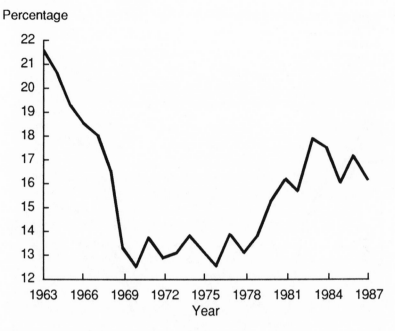

Source: See Figure 1.2

Figure 1.3   Low-Wage Shift—YRFT Workers (low wage = < $11,509 in 1987 dollars)

stagnation in the share during the 1970s, and then usually a large increase between 1979 and 1987.

The pattern of a shrinking middle found for the YRFT work force as a whole is particularly sharp for men, younger workers, those with less than a college degree, and workers in the Midwest where "deindustrialization" and high unemployment rates have apparently taken a greater toll. The U-turn exists, but is attenuated for older workers (age 35-54) and for those with a college degree. The major exception to the U-turn pattern is found among women, whose low-wage share plummeted between 1963 and 1973 and has remained at approximately the 1973 level ever since—a J-turn, so to speak, with no significant improvement after 1973.

ALTERNATIVE HYPOTHESES FOR THE U-TURN WAGE PATTERN

Finding similar U-turns in the real average wage, the variance in wages, and the low-wage share for so many demographic groups, in virtually all regions, and in

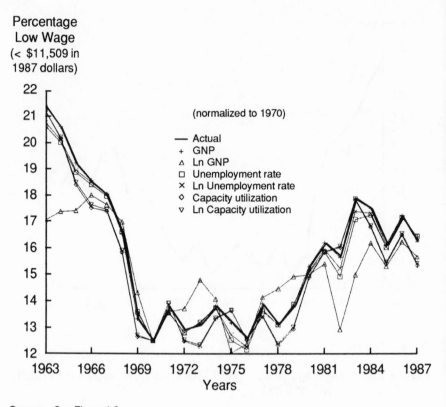

Source: See Figure 1.2

Figure 1.4   Low-Wage Share—YRFT Workers (actual vs. decycled data)

manufacturing as well as the service sector suggests the possibility of discovering a coherent source or set of factors to explain this distinctive pattern. At least five competing theories vie for this honor. They range from hypotheses about economic stagnation and business cycles to those that focus on changes in the demographics of the labor force, in the industrial composition of employment, and in the "institutional" environment that regulates the labor market. These alternative hypotheses can be summarized as follows.

The Business Cycle Hypothesis

The essential point underlying the business cycle hypothesis is that the alleged secular trends in wages and wage shares reflect nothing more than cyclical

Table 1.2   Distribution of Employment Levels for Year-Round, Full-Time Workers by Wage Strata, 1963, 1973, 1979, and 1987

Workers by Wage Level* & Other Characteristics	Shares of Total Employment			
	1963	1973	1979	1987
All YRFT Workers				
Low wage	21.4%	13.1%	13.8%	16.2%
Mid wage	75.5	78.7	78.3	75.3
High wage	3.1	8.1	7.9	8.5
By Gender				
Men				
Low wage	14.1%	7.4%	8.0%	11.5%
Mid wage	81.8	80.9	80.3	75.8
High wage	4.2	11.7	11.7	12.8
Women				
Low wage	41.3%	25.3%	24.2%	23.3%
Mid wage	58.6	74.1	74.7	74.7
High wage	0.1	0.6	1.0	2.1
By Race				
White				
Low wage	8.7%	11.8%	12.9%	15.1%
Mid wage	78.0	79.3	78.5	75.8
High wage	3.4	8.9	8.6	9.1
Nonwhite				
Low wage	48.6%	24.0%	20.9%	22.9%
Mid wage	51.4	74.1	76.4	72.7
High wage	0.1	1.9	2.8	4.4
By Age				
20-34				
Low wage	22.4%	13.7%	14.8%	19.8%
Mid wage	76.5	82.4	81.9	76.8
High wage	1.1	3.9	3.3	3.4
35-54				
Low wage	18.3%	10.0%	10.7%	11.6%
Mid wage	77.6	78.1	77.3	76.0
High wage	4.2	11.9	11.9	12.4
By Education				
Less than high school diploma				
Low wage	30.2%	21.1%	24.4%	32.6%
Mid wage	68.9	76.3	73.1	65.9
High wage	0.9	2.6	2.5	1.5
High school graduate				
Low wage	18.4%	13.3%	15.4%	19.7%
Mid wage	79.6	81.7	80.8	76.9
High wage	1.9	4.9	3.8	3.4
Some college				
Low wage	11.9%	9.3%	10.4%	17.5%
Mid wage	83.1	81.6	82.4	76.8
High wage	4.8	9.1	7.2	5.7

continued

Table 1.2   Continued

Workers by Wage Level* & Other Characteristics	Shares of Total Employment			
	1963	1973	1979	1987
College degree or more				
Low wage	9.6%	4.3%	4.7%	5.3%
Mid wage	78.2	72.8	74.3	73.7
High wage	12.2	22.9	21.0	21.0
By Region				
Northeast				
Low wage	16.9%	9.7%	11.4%	11.7%
Mid wage	79.6	81.0	80.3	78.2
High wage	3.5	9.3	8.3	10.1
Midwest				
Low wage	17.7%	11.6	12.0%	15.4%
Mid wage	79.7	80.2	80.2	77.0
High wage	2.6	8.2	7.8	7.5
South				
Low wage	33.6%	18.3%	18.0%	20.2%
Mid wage	64.2	75.3	75.4	72.7
High wage	2.2	6.5	6.6	7.0
West				
Low wage	13.9%	11.0%	12.0%	15.0%
Mid wage	81.5	79.6	78.0	74.5
High wage	4.7	9.4	10.0	10.4
By Employment				
Manufacturing				
Low wage	14.1%	9.6%	9.3%	11.9%
Mid wage	82.7	82.6	82.1	78.6
High wage	3.1	7.9	8.6	9.5
Services & trade				
Low wage	29.4%	17.3%	18.2%	20.3%
Mid wage	67.3	75.0	74.5	71.6
High wage	3.3	7.7	7.2	8.1

Source: Calculations from Annual Demographic Files, *Current Population Surveys*, March 1964, 1974, 1980, and 1988.

* Low wage = < $11,509/year; mid wage = $11,510–46,036/year; high wage = $46,037+ (in 1987 dollars)

phenomena having to do with normal expansions and contractions in the economy. As noted above, Janet Norwood (1987) is most explicit on this point in her critique of the original Bluestone and Harrison JEC study. She writes:

> Most of the studies done thus far . . . have attempted to find a long-term trend in the size of different wage groups. Our work at the Bureau of Labor Statistics suggests, however, that there is *a strong cyclical pattern that overwhelms any long-term trend.*

The lack of progress toward reducing low-wage employment reflects the impact of the 1981 to 1982 recession rather than a general inability of our economy to generate good jobs. We have nearly five years of earnings data for the recovery after the end of the 1973 to 1975 recession, but only three years (1983 to 1985) of data during the current recovery. Clearly we need more years of recovery to improve the situation. (p. F3; emphasis added)

According to this view, as the recovery continues, wages should rise as a result of ever-tightening labor markets. Firms bidding for labor will ultimately offer higher wages and the result will be a rise in average wages and a decline in the low-wage share of employment. Simply extending the economic recovery will therefore be sufficient to reverse the recent adverse U-turns.

The Stagnation Hypothesis

Closely related to the business cycle thesis is the theory that the decline in real average wages, and perhaps the growth in wage inequality, is due to a secular slowdown in the rate of productivity growth. Baily and Blair (1988) estimate growth in gross domestic product (GDP) per hour of labor in the entire economy and in manufacturing from 1950–86 in Table 1.3. According to the stagnation hypothesis, the long-term growth rate of earnings cannot exceed the long-term growth rate in productivity. Hence, the slowdown and even decline in real wages is directly attributable to the slowdown in productivity growth.

Table 1.3   Productivity Growth in the United States, 1950–87

Years	Growth of GDP per Hour		
	Total Economy	Manufacturing	Ratio
1950–73	2.44%	2.62%	1.07
1973–79	0.80	1.09	1.36
1979–86	1.09	3.10	2.84

Source: Baily and Blair (1988), Table 6-1, p. 180

An extension of this argument might explain growing wage dispersion. According to the Baily and Blair productivity estimates, the productivity growth differential between the manufacturing sector and the total economy has expanded dramatically since 1979. If workers' pay in each sector is determined by productivity in that sector, then diverging productivity—in this case between manufacturing and all other sectors—could be responsible for growing wage differentials.

The Demographic Hypothesis

Until quite recently, the most prevalent explanation for the slippage in average real wages and growth in the low-wage share of employment was underscored by two demographic trends: growth in female labor force participation and the coming of work force age of the baby boom generation. Robert Z. Lawrence (1984) of the Brookings Institution has been one of the most prominent of those suggesting that the crowding of a large cohort of relatively inexperienced workers into the labor market beginning in the late 1960s temporarily depressed wage levels. According to this thesis, the enormous increase in labor supply posed by the combination of baby boomers and a large number of women of all ages entering the labor force at the same time bid wages down for the entire economy and led to greater wage dispersion between younger, inexperienced workers and their older colleagues. With the baby boom generation gaining labor market experience and its successor, the baby bust generation, entering the labor market in smaller numbers, this trend should reverse as the result of normal supply and demand phenomena. Thus, in like manner to the business cycle hypothesis, the U-turn is regarded as a temporary phenomenon, presumably soon to be reversed.

"Deindustrialization" Hypothesis

Counterposed to both of the preceding hypotheses is "deindustrialization" theory. Its premise is that the observed U-turns in real wages and wage dispersion can best be explained by the shift in the economy from manufacturing to services (Bluestone and Harrison, 1982; Harrison and Bluestone, 1988). Accordingly, displacement of workers from the manufacturing sector has resulted in the destruction of generally higher wage jobs. In their place, the service and retail trade sectors of the economy have generated millions of new jobs, but they tend to be associated with a polarized earnings distribution with more low-wage employment being created than high-wage jobs. Unless there is a reversal in employment trends or substantial upgrading of jobs in services and trades, the deindustrialization hypothesis argues that stagnation in real wages, growth in the low-wage share, and polarization of the entire earnings distribution will continue, regardless of expected demographic trends and the normal business cycle.

The Institutional Hypotheses

Finally, there is a host of hypotheses about the effect of changes in labor market institutions on wage stagnation and earnings inequality. Chief among these factors are the decline in unionization and the falling value of the statutory minimum wage. In particular, Blackburn, Bloom, and Freeman (1989) argue that growing wage differentials between less educated and less skilled workers on one hand and more educated and more skilled workers on the other can be explained by the fact that trade unions and the minimum wage traditionally boosted the wages of the less educated and less skilled work force relative to those not unionized and those well above the minimum wage. With the recent decline in union strength and the erosion of the real value of the minimum wage, these institutional structures no longer enhance wages for many workers in the low end of the labor market.

This argument is similar to a much earlier one of Johnson and Youmans (1971) who demonstrate statistically that unionization of less educated workers substitutes for additional years of schooling in generating higher wage rates. Essentially, the presence of unions reduces overall wage inequality by augmenting the earnings of less schooled workers by a greater margin than workers with advanced educations. As a corollary, with the recent decline of union representation, the role of education in the wage determination process gains in relative importance. According to this hypothesis, to reduce overall wage inequality will require the restrengthening and expansion of unions, and for the lowest wage workers, an increase in the minimum wage.

TESTING THE FIVE HYPOTHESES

In the current debate over the causes of the U-turn in labor market outcomes, there is no single unified test of the hypotheses outlined above. Instead, for the most part, various investigators have attempted to assess the significance (or lack thereof) of one or another. While these studies have not provided a definitive answer to the roots of labor market U-turns, they have shed some light on the relative merit of each theory. Here we review much of the recent evidence.

Evidence on the Business Cycle and Demographic Hypotheses

Statistical tests provide little confirmation of the business cycle hypothesis or baby boom theory. As noted in Figure 1.4, decycling the YRFT low-wage share does nothing to remove the strong U-turn pattern in this series. Similarly, Harrison, Tilly, and Bluestone (1986) ran OLS regressions where the aggregate unemployment rate and the Federal Reserve Board's index of capacity utilization were used to ''decycle'' the VARLNWAGE for 1963 through 1983. After decycling, they found that ''the U-shaped pattern of inequality in individual wage and salary incomes becomes, if anything, even more pronounced'' (p. 29). When this research is carried out through 1987, precisely the same results are found. Decycling with any of six different cyclical variables—the aggregate unemployment rate, the natural log of the unemployment rate, deviations from the 1963–87 trend in GNP, the natural log of these deviations, and the level and log of capacity utilization—leaves the U-turn in VARLNWAGE virtually unchanged. Burtless (1989) comes to exactly the same conclusion for the years between 1967 and 1987. Regression results on the Gini coefficients on earnings for men and women suggest ''that very little if any of the fluctuation . . . has been due to cyclical factors'' (p. 22).

What makes these results that much more convincing is that the test of time Norwood (1987) suggests has failed to displace the U-turn pattern. Despite the continued economic recovery beyond 1985, average real wages continue to stagnate and the VARLNWAGE rose in both 1986 and 1987 (recall Figure 1.2). Similarly, while the rise in the YRFT low-wage share slowed after 1982, by 1987 the share was still more than three points higher than in 1978.

The one fragment of evidence suggesting that the business cycle does matter comes from regional data (Table 1.2). The region experiencing the lowest unemployment rate—the Northeast—had the slowest growth in low-wage share and the highest in the high-wage share of all regions. Not shown are results from New England which actually experienced a small decline in the low-wage share between 1979 and 1987. This finding may suggest that tight labor markets do increase wages and help reduce the low-wage share, but only when unemployment rates are pushed below 4 percent for a sustained period. The only period when this occurred nationwide was during the last four years of the 1960s when the aggregate jobless rate never exceeded 3.7 percent and fell to a low of 3.4 percent. Indeed, during this period the low-wage share fell substantially and wage dispersion was near its postwar minimum. We might conclude that normal economic growth consistent with a 5 percent or greater unemployment rate is at best sufficient to arrest further wage inequality but cannot reverse it.

Similarly, tests of the demographic hypotheses have yielded little support for these theories. Harrison, Tilly, and Bluestone (1986) used the proportion of the labor force under 35 as a proxy for the baby boom generation's entry into the labor market. Regressing VARLNWAGE on this variable and various measures of the business cycle for 1963 through 1983 once again left the U-turn intact. Likewise, Burtless (1989) finds that inequality has grown since 1967 in every age category for men while remaining essentially unchanged among women, suggesting that "generational crowding by itself cannot provide a complete explanation of growing inequality among men, for the trend is apparent even in the oldest age groups where no effect would be anticipated" (p. 27). In fact, Burtless's own simulations of the Gini coefficients for 1967 through 1987 indicate that a hypothetical Gini measured under the assumption of a constant population distribution (no change in the age distribution) yields a slightly larger increase in the Gini than the actual increase (1989, Table 4). Tilly, Bluestone, and Harrison (1987a) come to a similar conclusion using a variance decomposition method:

> As a general result, changes in the gender, race, and age composition of the labor force since 1978 explain virtually nothing of the increase in variance in wage and salary incomes between 1978 and 1984. Indeed, if we performed the experiment of permitting gender, race, and age composition as well as the relative mean wages of gender, race, and age groups to vary, *while holding the within-group variances constant*, the net effect would actually be a *decrease* in overall earnings variance. (p. 21)

Inspection of data on the age composition of the work force suggests why the Burtless and Tilly-Bluestone-Harrison results are not surprising. The baby boom generation was by the early 1980s already fully integrated into the prime age work force. The young, inexperienced cohort of the 1980s is not a baby boom cohort, but a small baby bust generation as indicated by the shrinkage in the work force share aged 16–24. Yet, despite the sharp decline in the labor supply of young, inexperienced workers and the growing experience of the baby boomers, average real wages, VARLNWAGE, and the YRFT low-wage share continued to grow right through the mid- to late 1980s. By now, if the demographic hypothesis were correct, the labor force experience of the baby boomers should have paid off in rising real average wages and a falling low-wage share. It has not.

The impact of rising female labor force participation on labor market outcomes is more complex and is dealt with in the next section.

Evidence on the Stagnation and Deindustrialization Hypotheses

Evidence is stronger for the stagnation and deindustrialization hypotheses, particularly in terms of the close agreement between patterns of productivity growth and the trend in real weekly earnings. The high rate of productivity growth during the period ending in 1973 (Table 1.3) corresponds to rapid growth in real weekly earnings (Figure 1.1). Similarly, the slowdown in productivity advance after 1973 corresponds to the decline in real wages while the small resurgence in productivity in the 1980s corresponds to the relative stability in real wages then.

This is not particularly surprising from a theoretical or accounting perspective. Unless there are major shifts in factor shares between labor and capital—for which there is little evidence—average real wage growth is constrained to the average growth in output per person hour worked. Hence the pattern in productivity growth and trends in real wage growth should be similar.

Of less certainty is the relationship between the trend in productivity and the U-turns in wage dispersion and the YRFT low-wage share. But when these patterns are studied, the links between productivity growth rates and these measures are maintained. The same thing is true for the deindustrialization hypothesis as proxied by the share of total employment in manufacturing.

I find evidence for these claims in three reduced-form, double $\log_e$ time-series OLS regressions for 1963–87. In Table 1.4, I display the results of separately regressing the CPI-X1 deflated real average weekly earnings data, the GNP-decycled VARLNWAGE time series, and the decycled YRFT low-wage share time series on productivity (ln output per hour); the log shares of the work force employed in manufacturing; and of the total work force aged 16–34 (as a measure of possible baby boom effect); and the female proportion of the work force (ln %FEMALE). For all its imperfections as a full specification, the model generates results that are reasonably consistent with standard labor market theory.

The productivity index has the expected sign in all three regressions. The estimate of near unit elasticity (1.09) in the real wage equation is extremely close to

Table 1.4   Determinants of Real Average Weekly Earnings, Decycled VARLNWAGE, and Low-Wage Employment Shares for Year-Round, Full-Time Workers, 1963–87

	Ln Real AWE	Ln VARLNWAGE	Ln Low-Wage Share
Constant	.225	5.33	12.22
	(.23)	(2.03)	(2.46)
Ln QperH	1.09	-1.21	-2.18
	(6.52)	(2.61)	(2.48)
Ln %MFG	.38	- .67	- .97
	(5.50)	(3.47)	(2.67)
Ln %AGE16–34	.39	- .96	-2.00
	(4.01)	(3.55)	(3.89)
Ln %FEMALE	-1.72	1.15	2.81
	(6.69)	(1.62)	(2.09)
R-bar^2	.90	.71	.69
SEE	.017	.047	.090
D.F.	20	20	20
D.W.	1.28	1.57	.95

(t-statistics in parentheses)

what would be predicted in theory: real wage trends map productivity trends on virtually a one-to-one basis. Moreover, the negative coefficients on the productivity term in the VARLNWAGE and low-wage share regressions suggest that the low-wage share and overall earnings inequality do indeed respond affirmatively to the pace of productivity growth. When productivity lags, wage dispersion and the low-wage share rise, especially with regard to the low-wage share which falls at a rate more than twice as fast as the rate at which productivity rises.[11]

The deindustrialization measure is also statistically significant in all three equations. Its positive sign in the real wage regression suggests that the reduced share of total employment in manufacturing has indeed contributed to stagnating wages. The negative signs in the VARLNWAGE and low-wage share equations add further evidence that the shift away from manufacturing employment towards a postindustrial service economy has been at least partially responsible for the increase in low-wage employment and the increase in wage inequality.

Some additional evidence bears on the deindustrialization hypothesis beyond the regression results. Table 1.5 contains estimates of the VARLNWAGE for all workers (age 16 and over) by broad industry grouping for 1979 and 1987. Inspection of the table reveals two phenomena. One is that, in general, the goods-producing

Table 1.5   Inequality within and among Industrial Sectors, 1979 and 1987

Industry	Variance in the Log of Annual Wages and Salaries		
	1979	1987	% Change
Mining	0.862	0.750	-13.0
Construction	1.491	1.526	+ 2.3
Durable manufacturing goods	0.849	0.809	-4.7
Nondurable manufacturing goods	1.220	1.251	+2.5
Transportation, communications & utilities	1.028	1.112	+8.2
Wholesale & retail trade	2.013	2.085	+3.6
Finance, insurance & real estate	1.274	1.364	+7.1
Business & repair services	1.933	2.241	+15.9
Entertainment & recreation services	2.208	2.613	+18.3
Professional services	1.584	1.661	+4.9

Source: Calculations from Annual Demographic Files, *Current Population Survey*, March 1980 and March 1988.

Note: Sample includes all workers aged 16 and over who had some wages during the year.

industries (mining, construction, durable and nondurable manufacturing) have traditionally had more equal wages than the service industries. The second is that wage inequality is rising significantly faster in the service sectors. The VARLNWAGE actually declined in mining and durable manufacturing during the 1980s and rose only modestly in construction and nondurable manufacturing. In contrast, all of the service sector industries had larger percentage increases in their wage dispersions than any of the goods-producing sectors.

Based on these findings, it would not be surprising that a growth in wage dispersion has accompanied the shift in aggregate employment from goods production to services. Employment has been stable or declining in the manufacturing industries where wage inequality is low, while it is growing rapidly in the services sector where it is considerably higher. While this shift does not automatically result in a higher overall variance measure and certainly cannot explain the entire U-turn in the labor market, it appears to play a not insignificant role especially in explaining the growth in inequality during the 1980s.

Returning to the regression results in Table 1.4 provides some insight into the demographic hypotheses. There seems to be little doubt from the real wage equation that the rise in women's labor force participation has been associated with stagnating average earnings. That women earn on average only 65 percent as much as men suggests that mathematically an increase in the female share of the overall work force will inevitably lead to a decline in the overall average wage even if men's and women's earnings are each rising individually. The positive coefficient in the low-wage share equation suggests the same phenomenon. In contrast, however, the role of female work force participation in explaining the U-turn in overall earnings variance is only weakly confirmed in the VARLNWAGE equation. The positive sign is consistent with this trend, but the low t-statistic on the coefficient provides little confidence that there is a compelling association between the size of the female share of the work force and wage inequality.

Finally, note that the coefficients on the baby boom term are all statistically significant, but each of their signs is "wrong." The expansion of the baby boom generation did not lead to falling average wages, to a larger dispersion in wages, or to a larger low-wage share. If anything, just the opposite seems to have occurred. During the period of the greatest expansion in the young work force—before 1979—real average wages were at their historic peak, while overall wage dispersion, and the low-wage share were both at their lowest point. In recent years, as the labor force of the 1970s aged and the baby boom was replaced by the baby bust generation, VARLNWAGE and the low-wage share actually rose while real wages declined. The timing of the baby boom and baby bust generations is simply inconsistent with the argument that changes in the size of age cohorts explain most labor market outcomes.

Evidence on the Institutional Labor Market Hypothesis

While the U-turns in real wages, wage dispersion, and the low-wage share have been shown to be associated with changes in productivity, the shift in industrial employment patterns, and the rise of female labor force participation, there is still some variance left to be explained. For one thing, the low-wage share has risen in the manufacturing sector of the economy as well as in services (recall Table 1.2). What can explain this universal pattern?

Blackburn, Bloom, and Freeman (1989) conclude that deunionization and the declining minimum wage are roughly as important as shifts in industry mix in explaining the growing wage gap between male high school dropouts and college graduates and between male blue-collar workers and professionals and managers. They find from regression analysis that "something on the order of a third of the fall in the relative earnings of the less skilled is associated with their moving from higher to lower paying industries and related industry-level factors" (p. 13). These are equivalent to the deindustrialization and stagnation variables used in the VARLNWAGE and low-wage share regressions in Table 1.4.

They also find, however, significant within-industry wage differentials that increase between 1979 and 1987.[12] These they subject to a pooled cross-section time-series regression analysis where the dependent variable is the log difference in annual earnings between high school dropouts and college graduate YRFT men in 43 industries. The independent variables include the percentage of industry employment consisting of men less than age 25, the proportions of women in the industry at various education levels, and the percentage of the work force unionized. In this regression, they find unionization is the only statistically significant factor explaining the wage differences between less schooled and highly schooled men. The higher the degree of unionization in an industry, the lower the wage differential. Further tests with this model, including factors for the rate of growth of labor productivity and the ratio of net imports to shipments, did not alter the compelling effect of unionization on earnings differentials.

A final investigation of institutional factors, using a sources-of-change analysis, was used to measure the proportion of the aggregate change in the earnings differential between male high school dropouts and college graduates attributable to industry mix, changes in the real value of the minimum wage, and changes in unionization (see Table 1.6). Blackburn and colleagues suggest that institutional factors plus industry shift phenomena explain more than two-thirds of the growing earnings differential between men of different education level. These results provide still additional evidence in favor of the deindustrialization and institutional hypotheses.

Table 1.6   Sources of Change Accounting Estimates of Determinants of the Decline in Relative Earnings of Less Skilled Men, 1973–87

	Ln Differential between High School Dropouts & College Graduates	
	All Men	*Men Aged 25–34*
Change in ln earnings differentials	-.14	-.20
Change due to:		
Industry mix	-.04	-.06
Minimum wage	-.02	-.02
Unionization	-.04	-.05
Total change explained	-.10	-.13
Percentage of change explained	71	65

Source: Blackburn, Bloom, and Freeman (1989), Table 10, p. 33.

Notes: Changes in earnings differentials are regression-corrected changes based on nine age dummies, eight regional dummies, and three marital status dummies. Changes in industry mix are shift-share decomposition changes with interactions excluded.

TOWARD A SYNTHESIS OF THE WAGE DISPERSION
AND LOW-WAGE SHARE ANALYSIS

In the final analysis, what factors explain the recent U-turns in the real wage, in VARLNWAGE, and in the low-wage share of total YRFT employment? The evidence presented here provides an initial basis for an answer to this question.

First, by way of summary, there is little evidence to support the business cycle hypothesis. If employment growth and declining unemployment were ever a significant factor in raising real wages and reducing wage dispersion, it has not been a critical factor in the 1970s and 1980s. Real average wages have not increased during the current economic expansion despite the aggregate unemployment rate's having fallen from 10.8 percent at the trough of the last recession to just about 5 percent at present. Moreover, virtually every indicator of wage dispersion and low-wage share has continued to show growth during the 1980s. If business cycle factors are to be more potent in reversing the U-turn, it appears unemployment rates will have to fall to 4 percent or less and be sustained there for a number of years.

Similarly, there appears to be little evidence to support the baby boom hypothesis. Again, the period since 1979 provides counterevidence. Precisely at a time when the number of young workers in the economy is steadily shrinking and the experience level of the overall labor force is growing (recall Table 1.1), wage dispersion is rising along with the size of the low-wage share. Moreover, the growth in the low-wage share—while disproportionately experienced by younger workers—was found for older, more experienced workers as well. Entrance of the baby bust generation into the labor force should have marked a slowdown in the low-wage share, yet just the opposite occurred.

There is more evidence for female labor force participation as a factor in the series of labor market U-turns. But even here the gender factor can explain only part of the trend in average wages and the low-wage share because of the timing of these trends. The low-wage share declined from 1963 to 1973 during a period in which the female share of the labor force was growing. In the following period, 1973 through 1979, the low-wage share stabilized despite the continuing increase in female labor force participation. Only after 1979 did the VARLNWAGE and the low-wage share increase, but ironically this was during a period in which the annual rise in the female share of total employment was beginning to slow. Consistent with these trends, the regression analyses presented in Table 1.4 demonstrated only a weak statistical relationship between the female share of the labor force and wage inequality as measured by VARLNWAGE.

A more likely story, then, is that other factors, particularly those related to labor demand and various institutional changes, share responsibility for the overall trends we have found in the labor market. The particular factors analyzed here included the slowdown in productivity growth, the decline in manufacturing employment, the decline in unionization, and the decline in the real value of the minimum wage. The preponderance of the evidence suggests that these are the key factors at work in the U-turns studied here. But is there some way to synthesize these factors into a coherent story?

Table 1.7 contains an important clue. Superficially, Table 1.7 demonstrates what most researchers now take for granted: the growing importance of formal education as a determinant of earnings. Note in the column labeled Ratio '87/'73 that the degree of wage erosion—measured as the ratio of mean real annual earnings in 1987 to those in 1973—is monotonically related to the level of schooling completed. By 1987, the real average wage for workers who did not complete high school had dropped to 77 percent of its 1973 value and for those with a high school degree, 89 percent. Essentially, only those with education beyond the high school diploma have been able to maintain their real mean earnings—at 97 percent of their 1973 value.

This information, which corroborates the differential growth in low-wage shares by education category demonstrated in Table 1.1, strongly suggests that the U-turn in overall wage inequality is related directly to the increasing rewards to college education and the increasing penalties attached to not completing high school. The indexed values in the right-hand panel of Table 1.7 show that in 1963, those with a college degree earned about 2.1 times as much as those who did not complete high school. By 1979, this ratio was still below 2.4. By 1987, however, the ratio was better than 2.9 and presumably growing. Overall, between 1963 and 1987, the size of the earnings differential had grown by nearly 38 percent. The growing importance of education found here is fully consistent with the work of Blackburn, Bloom, and Freeman (1989) reported above.

But Table 1.7 suggests an additional factor is at work underlying the growing significance of education, and this factor takes us back to the "deindustrialization" hypothesis. When the trend in earnings by education group is disaggregated by industry category, it becomes clear that the growing education differential we have found is mainly confined to the services sector. Note that in 1963 the earnings ratio between individuals with a college degree and those who did not complete high school was roughly equivalent in both the goods-producing and service sectors of the economy. The relevant ratios are 2.11 and 2.20, respectively. By 1987, the ratios have diverged substantially. In goods production, the ratio has increased by less than 15 percent to 2.42. In services, the ratio has mushroomed to 3.52, an increase of 60 percent.

How can we interpret these results? What seems to be true is that the decline in real wages and the growth in VARLNWAGE and the low-wage share in the economy are attributable to a complex of factors which begins within individual industries and interindustrial shifts in employment and is then ratified by the sharp educational differentials in the services sector. Elsewhere, my colleague Bennett Harrison and I have argued that attempts by U.S. corporations to cope with international competition during the late 1970s and throughout the 1980s led to a series of "lean and mean" strategies that reduced employment and forced wage reductions in many high-wage industries (Harrison and Bluestone, 1988). This would certainly help to explain the nearly $2,000 decline in real average wages between

Table 1.7   Mean Real Annual Earnings by Education and Industry for All Workers: 1963, 1973, 1979, 1987

Work Force	1963	1973	1979	1987	Ratio '87/'73	Indexed Values (<HS degree = 1.00) 1963	1973	1979	1987
Total Work Force	$14,584	$18,130	$17,287	$18,063					
By Industry									
Goods producing	$18,315	$21,689	$21,203	$19,864					
Services	13,189	16,085	15,270	16,615					
By Education Group									
Less than HS degree	$11,486	$12,995	$11,407	$10,039	0.773	1.000	1.000	1.000	1.000
High school degree	15,381	18,276	16,772	16,191	0.886	1.339	1.406	1.470	1.613
Some college	15,618	17,513	16,715	16,939	0.967	1.360	1.348	1.465	1.687
College degree or more	24,231	29,999	27,248	29,213	0.974	2.110	2.309	2.389	2.910 37.94%
By Education and Industry									
Goods Producing									
Less than HS degree	$15,676	$17,737	$16,104	$13,768	0.776	1.000	1.000	1.000	1.000
High school degree	18,968	21,884	20,910	19,087	0.872	1.210	1.234	1.298	1.386
Some college	21,062	22,152	22,168	20,718	0.935	1.344	1.249	1.377	1.505
College degree or more	33,144	38,460	35,577	33,367	0.868	2.114	2.168	2.209	2.424 14.62%
Services									
Less than HS degree	$9,863	$10,096	$8,642	$7,798	0.772	1.000	1.000	1.000	1.000
High school degree	13,616	15,826	14,246	14,365	0.908	1.380	1.568	1.648	1.842
Some college	13,300	15,136	14,298	15,167	1.002	1.348	1.499	1.654	1.945
College degree or more	21,697	27,217	24,879	27,446	1.008	2.200	2.696	2.879	3.520 60.00%

Source: Calculations from the Annual Demographic Files, *Current Population Surveys*, March 1964–March 1988

Notes: Goods Producing: mining, construction, durable manufacturing, and nondurable manufacturing; Services: transportation, communications, utilities, wholesale and retail trade; finance, insurance, and real estate; business and repair services, entertainment and recreation services, and professional services

1973 and 1987 *within* the goods-producing sector (see Table 1.7) and the increase in manufacturing's low-wage share as shown in Table 1.2.[13]

But the changes taking place within the services sector are probably of even greater import and help to explain the overall growth in wage inequality. The high VARLNWAGE figures we found in such industries as wholesale and retail trade, business and repair services, entertainment and recreation services, and professional services (recall Table 1.4) are apparently attributable to the sizable school-related wage differentials in these sectors. Hence, as the economy transfers workers from goods production where schooling-related wage differentials are relatively low to the service industries where such differentials are high, the overall degree of wage inequality is destined to increase.

What chance is there then that wage inequality will decrease in the future? Given this analysis, three factors could reverse the wage dispersion trend. One would be the "reindustrialization" of the economy—a significant resurgence of employment in the goods-producing industries. This change would move workers into industries which have a higher mean annual wage at every schooling level and industries in which wage variance because of education is relatively small. The second factor would be a significant increase in educational opportunity for those workers who would otherwise not go beyond high school. Reducing the variance in education by substantially increasing college attendance would presumably reduce wage variance in the service sector and thus contribute to overall wage equality. Finally, the greater wage dispersion in service industries could be reduced by altering the institutional structure of these industries. To the extent that unionization tends to provide for greater wage equalization within an industry—within and across schooling categories—a greater union presence in the service sector could lead to somewhat smaller wage differentials.

It seems doubtful that any of these scenarios will come to pass in the near future. The trend away from manufacturing employment, while temporarily slowing because of an increased export market, does not show any evidence of reversing. Union organizing drives in the service economy are gaining some momentum, but growth in union membership is well below growth in employment. As for expanding education—perhaps the best hope for reversing the U-turn—the problem seems not to be a lack of commitment, but a lack of funds. To prepare more students for higher education will require better primary and secondary schools and this will in turn necessitate greater public spending. Moreover, with the cost of a college education rising faster than overall inflation, it is becoming more difficult for working class and low-income individuals to afford postsecondary education. New sources of college and university finance will need to be developed to bring down the pecuniary barriers to the college degree.

What is overwhelmingly clear from the sum total of the analysis is that the U-turns in real wages, in wage dispersion, and in low-wage shares will not automatically reverse simply as a result of a more benign business cycle or changes in labor market demographics. More than likely, various forms of investment in the economy in new manufacturing industries and in education, as well as the pursuit of direct measures to reduce wage inequality through unionization and improved minimum wage legislation—will be necessary to limit the growth in inequality in the U.S. labor market.

Notes

Bennett Harrison, Larry Mishel, and Chris Tilly kindly provided comment and criticism of an earlier draft.

1. Strictly speaking, the statistics did not refer to "jobs" per se, but to the number of workers employed. In fact, the number of new jobs likely exceeded the 20 million figure because of "moonlighting" by workers who package two or more part-time jobs during the workweek.

2. Much of the critique of the original JEC study was responsible and well-reasoned, particularly that of Janet L. Norwood (1987) and Marvin Kosters and Murray Ross (1987, 1988) in a series of papers for the American Enterprise Institute. Suggestions from these critics for improving the measurement of wage distributions—including the isolation of year-round, full-time workers; the use of "smoothed" medians; implementation of controls for the business cycle; and the need for closer examination of the price deflators used in the analysis—were all incorporated in later versions of the JEC-initiated research. To be sure, there were also outbursts of less well-intentioned responses. In this category, I would particularly single out Warren T. Brookes (1987) and Robert Samuelson (1987).

3. The year-round, full-time share of the work force has a strong cyclical component to it—rising during economic expansions and contracting during recessions as a result of layoffs and short workweeks. However, underlying the cycle is a slow upward trend of approximately 1.3 percentage points per decade, according to time-series regression analysis.

4. A declining average wage does not mean, of course, that the real wage for any particular individual or for any specific job has necessarily been falling. Age-earnings profiles for individuals and wages for existing jobs still tend to rise over time—although at a much smaller rate in the late 1970s and 1980s than during earlier periods. What the declining average suggests is that the composition of jobs in the labor market is shifting, with a disproportionate number of higher wage jobs disappearing while a disproportionate number of newly created jobs pay lower wages.

5. For the record, we should note that while there is little dispute as to the U-turn in real earnings, there is some disagreement about whether earnings is the correct statistic to measure. McKenzie (1988, p. 122) argues, for example, that there has been no U-turn at all in total compensation—wages including the value of job benefits such as health insurance, FICA payments, and private pensions. While this may be true, one should note that the expansion in nonwage job benefits is almost exclusively to cover the extraordinary increases in the cost of health insurance and social security payments. To measure the real dollar value of total compensation adequately, it would be necessary to use different price indices for wages and benefits. McKenzie or other critics of the U-turn have not done so. As it is, using standard inflation adjustment indices, Lawrence Mishel and Jaqueline Simon (1988) find that since 1979, even measures of total compensation per hour show virtually no growth.

6. To be sure, not all research has come to the same conclusion. Bradley Reiff (1986), working at M.I.T., using an earnings series that included self-employment income as well

as wages, found that for year-round, full-time men and women combined, there was a slight decrease in *weekly earnings* inequality between 1968 and 1983. Similarly, James Medoff (1984) at Harvard found a small decrease in *hourly earnings* inequality between 1973 and 1984. No definitive reason for these contradictory results has yet been discovered, but some researchers believe they can be traced to the particular samples chosen.

7. Discovery of a U-turn in the VARLNWAGE for all workers is not necessarily inconsistent with Burtless's finding of a long-term secular rise in wage inequality for men or women separately. Adding two distributions together can yield virtually any other distribution. In this particular case, our own analysis done separately for men and women yields two distinctly different patterns: secularly rising inequality for men à la Burtless and a shallow U-turn for women. For men, the VARLNWAGE in 1987 was nearly 12 percent higher than in 1963. For women, it is more than 10 percent lower, but higher than its mid-1970s level. Together, however, the two distributions yield a sharp U-turn in the variance in the log of earnings, declining by 14 percentage points between 1963 and 1978 while subsequently rising by more than 8 percentage points by 1987.

VARLNWAGE TRENDS BY SEX

Year	VARLNWAGE All	Men	Women	1963 Indexed Values All	Men	Women
1963	1.977	1.471	2.125	1.000	1.000	1.000
1964	1.999	1.494	2.143	1.011	1.016	1.008
1965	1.910	1.408	2.021	0.966	0.957	0.951
1966	1.825	1.342	1.921	0.923	0.912	0.904
1967	1.809	1.354	1.867	0.915	0.920	0.879
1968	1.789	1.343	1.847	0.905	0.913	0.869
1969	1.804	1.357	1.858	0.912	0.923	0.874
1970	1.848	1.428	1.890	0.935	0.971	0.889
1971	1.796	1.408	1.838	0.908	0.957	0.865
1972	1.790	1.397	1.821	0.905	0.950	0.857
1973	1.782	1.402	1.770	0.901	0.953	0.833
1974	1.760	1.401	1.754	0.890	0.952	0.825
1975	1.725	1.380	1.729	0.873	0.938	0.814
1976	1.732	1.411	1.717	0.876	0.959	0.808
1977	1.730	1.426	1.700	0.875	0.969	0.800
1978	1.704	1.395	1.685	0.862	0.948	0.793
1979	1.795	1.430	1.852	0.908	0.972	0.872
1980	1.781	1.471	1.814	0.901	1.000	0.854
1981	1.786	1.536	1.755	0.903	1.044	0.826

VARLNWAGE TRENDS BY SEX, continued

Year	VARLNWAGE All	Men	Women	1963 Indexed Values All	Men	Women
1982	1.881	1.471	1.814	0.951	1.000	0.854
1983	1.934	1.724	1.917	0.978	1.172	0.902
1984	1.884	1.624	1.910	0.953	1.104	0.899
1985	1.829	1.579	1.867	0.925	1.073	0.879
1986	1.843	1.606	1.872	0.932	1.092	0.881
1987	1.865	1.641	1.902	0.943	1.116	0.895

Source: Annual Demographic Files, *Current Population Surveys*, March 1964–March 1988.

8. The year 1973 represents the postwar year in which real average weekly earnings peaked. Hence, all years are compared against the year in which real wages were a maximum.

9. This produces real wage cutoffs (in 1987 dollars) equivalent to: low-wage < $11,509; middle wage $11,509–$46,036; high wage $46,037+.

10. This decycling is a two-step regression procedure of the following form: (1) Decycling variable$_t$ = a_{0t} + a_{1t} Time + e_{1t} and (2) low-wage share$_t$ = b_{0t} + $b_{1t}e_{1t}$ + e_{2t}.

11. From a theoretical perspective, this result is fully anticipated in the case of the low-wage share. After all, the low-wage series used here reflects changes in the real wage as well as changes in distribution. The significant negative coefficient on VARLNWAGE has a weaker theoretical foundation since this series reflects purely distribution phenomena and no real wage effect. Why should changes in productivity growth affect the distribution of earnings? One possible explanation is that the pattern within the productivity series proxies for the shift over time in employment from the higher productivity manufacturing sector to the lower productivity growth services sector. Additional research is needed to confirm this hypothesis.

12. In a comparable study using a standard variance decomposition method, Tilly, Bluestone, and Harrison (1987a) estimate that 78 percent of the change in wage and salary earnings inequality among all workers has been associated with within-industry factors. The remainder is associated with interindustry employment shifts. Hence, restructuring of the labor market within industries is clearly important in its own right along with "deindustrialization."

13. Murphy and Welch (1988) provide some interesting corroborative evidence for these findings. Focusing on import competition as a contributing factor to a decline in manufacturing employment, they conclude that:

> Increases in import competition have strong negative impacts on wages for the unskilled: those with low levels of education and low levels of experience. In contrast relative wages for those with more experience and those with more education increase substantially with a rise in durable imports. (p. 51)

Hence, as durable imports rose, partly displacing domestic manufacturing, there was a downward shift on the wages of blue-collar workers with presumably little education and an upward shift in the wages of those with professional credentials and experience.

References

Baily, Martin Neil and Margaret M. Blair (1988) "Productivity and American Management." In *American Living Standards. Threats and Challenges*, edited by Robert E. Litan, Robert Z. Lawrence, and Charles L. Schultze, 178–214. Washington, DC: The Brookings Institution.

Blackburn, McKinley L. and David E. Bloom (1987) "Earnings and Income Inequality in the United States." *Population and Development Review* 13:575–609.

Blackburn, McKinley L., David E. Bloom, and Richard B. Freeman (1989) "Why Has the Economic Position of Less-Skilled Male Workers Deteriorated in the United States?" Brookings Discussion Papers in Economics. Washington, DC: The Brookings Institution.

Bluestone, Barry and Bennett Harrison (1982) *The Deindustrialization of America: Plant Closings, Community Abandonment, and the Dismantling of Basic Industries*. New York: Basic Books.

Bluestone, Barry and Bennett Harrison (1986) "The Great American Job Machine: The Proliferation of Low Wage Employment in the U.S. Economy. A Study Prepared for the Joint Economic Committee, The Congress of the United States. Boston: University of Massachusetts/Boston.

Bluestone, Barry and Bennett Harrison (1988), "The Growth of Low-Wage Employment: 1963–78." *American Economics Review* 78(2):124–28.

Brock, William E. (1987) "They're Not 'McJobs'." *Washington Post* (11 June):A23.

Brookes, Warren T. (1987) "Low-Pay Jobs: The Big Lie." *Wall Street Journal* (25 March):30.

Burtless, Gary (1989) "Earnings Inequality over the Business Cycle." Brookings Discussion Papers in Economics. Washington, DC: The Brookings Institution.

Dooley, Martin D. and Peter Gottschalk (1982) "Does a Younger Male Labor Force Mean Greater Earnings Inequality?" *Monthly Labor Review* 105(11):42–45.

Dooley, Martin D. and Peter Gottschalk (1984) "Earnings Inequality among Males in the United States: Trends and the Effect of Labor Force Growth." *Journal of Political Economy* 92:59–89.

Grubb, W. Norton and Robert H. Wilson (1986) "The Distribution of Wages and Salaries, 1960–1980: The Contribution of Gender, Race, Sectoral, and Regional Shifts." Paper presented at the conference of the Association for Public Policy Analysis and Management, October.

Harrison, Bennett and Barry Bluestone (1987) "The Dark Side of Labour Market 'Flexibility': Falling Wages and Growing Income Inequality in America." Labour Market Analysis and Employment Planning Working Paper no. 17. World Employment Programme Research Working Papers. WEP 2-43/WP. 17. Geneva: International Labour Office.

Harrison, Bennett and Barry Bluestone (1988) *The Great U-Turn: Corporate Restructuring and the Polarizing of America.* New York: Basic Books.

Harrison, Bennett, Chris Tilly, and Barry Bluestone (1986). ''Wage Inequality Takes a Great U-Turn.'' *Challenge* 29(1):26–32.

Henle, Peter and Paul Ryscavage (1980) ''The Distribution of Earnings among Men and Women, 1958-1977.'' *Monthly Labor Review* 103(4):3–10.

Johnson, George E. and Kenwood C. Youmans (1971) ''Union Relative Wage Effects by Age and Education.'' *Industrial and Labor Relations Review* 24:171–79.

Kosters, Marvin H. and Murray N. Ross (1987) ''The Distribution of Earnings and Employment Opportunities: A Re-examination of the Evidence.'' American Enterprise Institute Occasional Papers. Washington, DC: American Enterprise Institute.

Kosters Marvin H. and Murray N. Ross (1988) ''The Quality of Jobs: Evidence from Distributions of Annual Earnings and Hourly Wages.'' Washington, DC: American Enterprise Institute.

Lawrence, Robert Z. (1984) ''Sectoral Shifts and the Size of the Middle Class.'' *The Brookings Review* 3(1):3–11.

Loveman, Gary W. and Chris Tilly (1988) ''Good Jobs or Bad Jobs: What Does the U.S. Evidence Say?'' *New England Economic Review* (January/February):46–65.

McKenzie, Richard B. (1988) *The American Job Machine.* New York: Universe Books.

Medoff, James L. (1984) ''The Structure of Hourly Earnings among U.S. Private Sector Employees: 1973-1984.'' New York: National Bureau of Economic Research.

Mishel, Lawrence (1988) ''Better Jobs or Working Longer for Less: An Evaluation of the Research of Marvin Kosters and Murray Ross of the Quality of Jobs.'' Economic Policy Institute Working Paper no. 101. Washington, DC.

Mishel, Lawrence and Jaqueline Simon (1988) ''The State of Working America.'' *Challenge* 31(6):50–51.

Murphy, Kevin and Finis Welch (1988) ''The Structure of Wages.'' University of Chicago Working Paper. Chicago.

Norwood, Janet L. (1987) ''The Job Machine Has Not Broken Down.'' *New York Times* (22 February):F3.

Reiff, Bradley (1986) ''Industry and Occupation Employment Structure and Income Distribution.'' Cambridge: Department of Economics, Massachusetts Institute of Technology.

Rosenthal, Neal H. (1985) "The Shrinking Middle Class: Myth or Reality." *Monthly Labor Review* 108(3):3–10.

Samuelson, Robert (1987) "The American Job Machine." *Newsweek* 109 (23 February):57.

Tilly, Chris, Barry Bluestone, and Bennett Harrison (1987a) "The Reasons for Increasing Wage and Salary Inequality, 1978–1984." John W. McCormack Institute of Public Affairs Working Paper. Boston: University of Massachusetts at Boston.

Tilly, Chris, Barry Bluestone, and Bennett Harrison (1987b) "What is Making American Wages More Unequal?" *Industrial Relations Research Association Series. Proceedings of the Thirty-Ninth Annual Meeting, December 28–30, 1986, New Orleans*, edited by Barbara D. Dennis, 338-57. Madison, WI: Industrial Relations Research Association.

U.S. Senate, Committee on the Budget Staff (1988). "Wages of American Workers in the 1980s." Washington, D.C.: Committee on the Budget, U.S. Senate, Congress of the United States.

COMMENT

Thomas J. Plewes

The special problem of my discussion is that it is sandwiched between Bluestone and Kosters who agree on only one thing—they both use Bureau of Labor Statistics (BLS) data to prove their diametrically opposed viewpoints.

As a reviewer, I must begin by suggesting that you read Bluestone's chapter. He has succinctly, if not entirely convincingly, captured the essence of the arguments over one of the great debates of the day. If I say not entirely convincingly, for reasons that I want to stress in this discussion, I should go on to say that what we have heard today is far more convincing than what we have heard before. It is possible that we are seeing a convergence of analysis that may well lead to convergence of policy response. So what we have heard today is quite important in that respect.

It is fitting that I discuss this important chapter under the auspices of the Center for Competitiveness and Employment Growth. There can be little doubt, looking at employment and production figures, that we are in a period of unusually sustained growth. This growth is occurring in an era of intense competition for domestic and international markets.

Indeed, I claim that the competition is even more pervasive than this chapter might credit. The U-turn is now quite clearly documented. This trend in earnings, at least for men, is one manifestation of a much more intense economic competition that has made itself increasingly evident. It is not the only one. Competitive strategies also include increasing use of temporary and part-time employees, contracting out, contingent work arrangements, and employee ''leasing.''

These developments suggest increasing flexibility of the work force. There are benefits—the ability of many workers to combine work and family obligations better, the potential for the economy to sustain economic growth with lesser risks of inflationary spiral, and increased competitiveness in product markets as a result of reduced labor costs. But there are also costs. The ''shift toward contingent workers,'' as Richard S. Belous (1979) points out, produces economic insecurity among the contingent sectors of the labor force, increases the level and rate at which unemployment might rise in recession, and discourages employers' investment in human capital.

Some point out that contingent workers may be paid less than ''core workers'' for doing similar jobs. That, of course, would be one more factor behind the decline in average real earnings.

39

But even as this situation extends the evidence of competition beyond earnings issues, the competitive forces extend their impact beyond the hypotheses Professor Bluestone presents. For example, he suggests that the deindustrialization hypothesis is one of the more valuable tools for understanding real wage stagnation and increasing wage inequality. However, wage stagnation—or a U-turn in earnings—transcends industrial sectors.

Manufacturing wages—as measured by real average hourly earnings, excluding overtime—have made a U-turn of their own. As we can see in Figure 1A.1, that measure has clearly paralleled the weekly earnings data of Professor Bluestone, although with a lag of a few years.

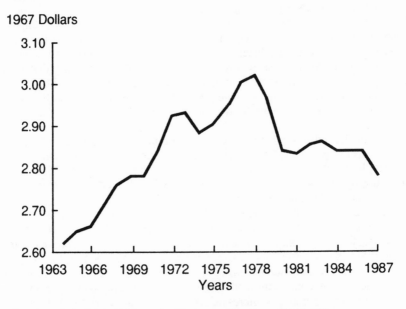

Figure 1A.1   The U-Turn in Factory Wages, 1964–87

It is interesting to speculate on what a similar measure of hourly "wage" for all nonfarm workers, also stripped of the cyclical influences of overtime and work hours and the structural impacts of any shift toward part-time work, would show. My own guess is that the timing would more closely match the factory wage series I computed here.

In fact, the real weekly earnings series for manufacturing, with overtime and the relatively long factory workweek included, also shows a peak in the late 1970s that had not been regained by 1987. In any case, the fact of a U-turn in manufacturing straight-time wages detracts from the utility of the deindustrialization hypothesis as a basis for understanding and responding to increased competitive pressures.

Bluestone's second important topic is a reported increase in wage inequality. He presents an informative consolidation of previous work on personal earnings inequality. However, there may be some specific methodological problems in Professor Bluestone's approach.

For example, what is more interesting—the behavior of the aggregate trend in the variance of the log of annual earnings (VARLNWAGE) or the strikingly different behaviors in the data disaggregated by sex that underlie that trend? Using the data Bluestone provides in a note, I have portrayed the disaggregated VARLNWAGE series in Figure 1A.2. My reading of that graph suggests that prior to 1978 the combination of declining inequality of earnings among women, essentially unchanged inequality among men, and a rapidly increasing labor force share for women yielded the 1963–78 downtrend in aggregate inequality illustrated in Professor Bluestone's Figure 1.2.

After 1978, both series break sharply upward in their measures of earnings inequality. That double upswing produced the rising trend in inequality since 1978. My supposition is that this 10-year period of parallel trends weakens the regres-

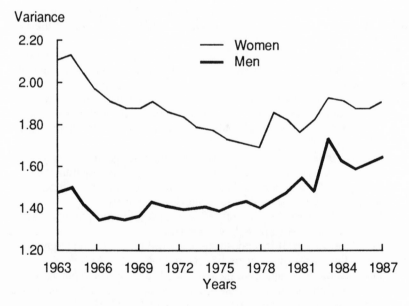

Figure 1A.2   Variance of Ln Annual Earnings, 1963–87

sion coefficients presented in Bluestone's Table 1.4 for the female share of the labor force as an explanatory variable.

It would be useful to test this hypothesis of a behavioral change in the way women have influenced wage inequality as their labor force participation rose. A dummy variable specification for the post-1978 period would be one approach. The post-1978 era, it seems to me, is where the action is. From my perspective, of course, the first question becomes, What changes, if any, were made in the way data are gathered and presented for public use during that time? In this case, the answer is interesting.

In 1981 and 1984, the "top-codes" for earnings data collected and data released were raised significantly. (The two are not the same because of the Census Bureau's confidentiality policies.) A higher top-coding by itself could lead to higher measured variances. It would have been technically interesting to read a footnote on Professor Bluestone's handling of this issue.

A substantive question to address in the post-1978 period is clear from the U-turn (albeit a shallow one) in the wage share analysis. The wage share analysis is based on the change in the share of the labor force made up of those in the lowest earnings category as defined by a constant dollar wage of half the median annual earnings in the base year. These are all measures that are not much affected by the top-coding problem.

These points raise some interesting technical issues of their own. Work by BLS staff on distributions of family income demonstrates the need for detailed sensitivity analyses for this mode of research. The sensitivity of the findings to the choice of earnings cutoffs and earnings deflator is a potential trouble spot. Horrigan and Haugen, in their 1988 *Monthly Labor Review* article, found their results to be extremely sensitive to the latter factor.

In summary, recent trends in real average earnings reflects, in part, the intensification of competition throughout the domestic and international economies. Further reflections of these competitive pressures are seen in manufacturing wages and the emergence of new human resource strategies—in particular the shift toward a more flexible work force. These trends are pervasive and may not be especially amenable to such sectoral analysis or prescription as the deindustrialization analysis presented here.

The analysis of trends in wage inequality is also interesting, but similarly needs some sharpening. As specific suggestions, I recommend disaggregating the variance of earnings study (and double checking the top-coding issue) and performing a rigorous sensitivity test on the low-wage-share analysis.

So, after all of this, where are we left? Bluestone would return to his wonderful days of yesteryear by specific policy responses:

● **Reindustrialization.** If this does take place, wouldn't new manufacturing be quite unlike the old? And if it were like the old, would it survive?

● **Reunionization.** If the unions of the future are like the growing unions today, a number of items are on their agenda beside raising wages. Job security and strengthening fringe benefits are certainly up there on their lists.

● **Minimum wage increases**. An immediate surge might be expected, but are the lasting effects clear?

No, we are left with only two pillars on which we might rebuild from Bluestone's vision of ashes. The need for a flexible response to the competitive pressures we are facing as a nation and in individual industries and areas is one. The other is increasingly obvious also. Education is at once the key and the problem. In pointing out this fact, Bluestone makes his most significant contribution.

References

Belous, Richard S. (1989) *The Contingent Economy: The Growth of the Contemporary Part-Time and Subcontracted Workforce*. NPA Report no. 239. Washington, DC: National Planning Association.

Horrigan, Michael W. and Steven E. Haugen (1988). "The Declining Middle-Class Thesis: A Sensitivity Analysis." *Monthly Labor Review* 111(5): 3-13.

2 THE OUTLOOK FOR JOBS AND LIVING STANDARDS

Marvin H. Kosters

In recent years there has been an upsurge of interest in labor market issues. There have been many studies and news stories on job creation and wages, on how well the typical worker or family has fared, on whether the distribution of wages or income has changed, and if so, why changes have occurred. Studies have been made of what has happened in the past and there has been speculation about trends in the future.

What accounts for the upsurge of interest in these questions? One reason, of course, is that many changes have occurred, and not all have been favorable. For one thing, real earnings have not increased as rapidly during the past 15 or 20 years as they did earlier. Some workers and communities have had serious setbacks. And we are in a transition from rapid growth in the work force to slower growth in the future, with a smaller share of future growth accounted for by U.S.-born white male workers.

For the economy as a whole, even though we have had strong increases in employment and much lower inflation in the 1980s, we also have a large federal budget deficit. In addition, our big trade deficit needs to be financed by borrowing about $10 billion a month from abroad. These circumstances give rise to legitimate concerns, not only about recent performance but also about prospects for the future.

Much of the rise of interest in labor market issues, however, probably stems from differences in perspectives on appropriate policy directions. National economic policy has generally been viewed as moving in a more market-oriented direction during the 1980s. Although the degree of movement in this direction should not be exaggerated, there has been more emphasis on broadening the scope for individual decisions while narrowing that for administrative action by government. There has been more reliance on prices and markets and less on regulation (see Henderson, n.d.).[1] As a consequence, developments in the labor market during the 1980s have sometimes been featured in national political debate.

Much of the interest in analyzing and interpreting recent history as it concerns jobs and pay has its roots, I believe, in the presumed implications for policy. In any event, one reason why I review several aspects of recent labor market performance is that I think what has actually occurred has sometimes been misunderstood. The second reason is that I interpret recent labor market trends as consistent with the view that more market-oriented policies have contributed to better performance instead of detracting from it.

Interpreting history, even recent history, is often accompanied by disagreement. This phenomenon is suggested by the variety one sees in familiar quotations about the role of history. Many learned quotations celebrate what we can learn from history. Some, however, disparage it, most notably Henry Ford, who said, "History is bunk!" Since the interpretation I place on recent labor market developments is more favorable than that of some others, I hope it doesn't produce a reaction suggested by a quip attributed to Leo Tolstoy: "History would be a wonderful thing—if only it were true."

INDIVIDUAL WORKERS' PAY

Trends in pay for individual workers can be examined in terms of how the typical worker has fared and whether pay is becoming more or less equally distributed. Both aspects of workers' pay have received considerable discussion during the past few years, and both have been used to characterize what has happened to the quality of jobs. For each aspect, different views have been expressed about what has actually been happening and why changes have occurred. In my discussion I draw on official statistics and on the research of others as well as my own to sketch out the main features of wage and income trends (see Kosters, 1988a).

A major reason for wide differences in interpretation of recent developments is that data can be assembled that seem to show quite different trends. Data are available for different earnings concepts and for various components of the work force, with breakdowns by industry, occupation, age, schooling, work status, and other characteristics. In addition, inflation needs to be taken into account to compare changes over time, and different official measures can be used. Selection of particular years for making comparisons can also influence apparent trends. Drawing on different data and combining them in various ways can lead to quite different conclusions about how workers have been faring.

The many possibilities for making statistical comparisons can lead to confusion or skepticism about whether it is possible to arrive at straightforward answers to simple questions. But the availability of extensive data should help to enrich our understanding of developments in the labor market. When different measures suggest different trends, discussion of why divergent results are obtained can contribute insights into the more subtle changes that have occurred.

Workers' Average Pay

Rising real incomes during the 1950s and 1960s generated public confidence that such increases could be expected to continue. That confidence was shaken during the 1970s, when many probably felt that inflation was cheating them out of increases in real earnings that they could otherwise legitimately expect. Although the big decline in inflation in the early 1980s was not accompanied by a corresponding surge in real income growth, output per hour of work may be increasing somewhat more rapidly than during most of the 1970s.

It is generally recognized that productivity growth has been slower since the early 1970s than before and that this slowdown was experienced by all the major industrial economies. This productivity slowdown is the most important feature affecting long-term comparisons of changes in real earnings. Real output per hour of work has increased, but more slowly than before. Since 1973 it has increased by 12.5 percent, with most of the increase coming since 1980.

Even the relatively simple question of whether workers have on average received increases in pay, after adjusting for inflation, depends on the data chosen to answer it. This situation is clear from the data charted in Figure 2.1 that include some of the most commonly used measures of average pay.

One important difference in these data series is the measure of prices used to adjust for inflation. Average hourly and weekly earnings are charted as they are usually reported using the consumer price index (CPI) to adjust for inflation. The method for measuring the housing costs' component of the CPI was changed at the beginning of 1983, however, and the effects of this change in definition are taken into account in the middle series (CPI-U-X1). This adjusted CPI represents a consistent measure of price changes over time by eliminating an overstatement prior to 1983 of the effects of inflation on average living standards (see Horrigan and Haugen, 1988; *Monthly Labor Review* Staff, 1985). The top two series are adjusted for inflation by using the personal consumption expenditures deflator (PCE), a measure similar in concept and in overall trend to the adjusted CPI.

Conceptual differences in what these various series measure are also important. The stronger downtrend in average weekly earnings, for example, reflects the gradual reduction over time in average weekly hours of work—from 36.9 in 1973 to 34.8 in 1987. Apparently this long-term decline in average working hours reflects mainly workers' choices; shorter normal working hours are increasingly common, and more than two-thirds of part-time work is voluntary. A major deficiency of weekly earnings as a measure of how the average worker has been faring is that it reflects changes in time spent at work as well as changes in rates of pay.

Real per capita income, is deficient as a measure of the typical worker's pay for two reasons. First, this measure of income covers more than labor earnings; it also includes income such as pensions, transfers, interest, dividends, and rent. Second,

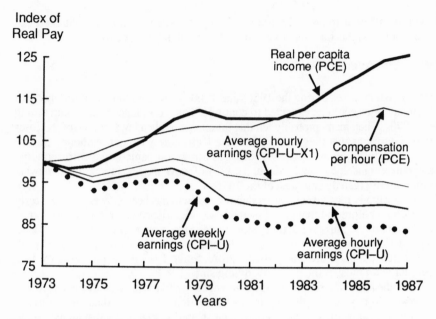

Source: *Economic Report of the President, 1988*, Tables B-45, B-44, B-47; *Money Income of Households, Families and Persons in the U.S., 1986*, Current Population Reports, Series P-60, no. 159, Table 28.

Figure 2.1   Measures of Real Pay, 1973–87

it reflects changes in the fraction of the population employed as well as changes in their rate of pay. The ratio of employment to the working-age population, for example, has increased from 57.8 percent in 1973 to 61.5 percent in 1987, largely as a result of the rising fraction of women in the work force. Like average weekly earnings, real per capita income shows a noticeable cyclical pattern. Its pronounced rise reflects the strong rise in employment during most of the past 15 years and the decline in unemployment by 1987 to a rate lower than at any time since the early 1970s.

Compensation per hour and average hourly earnings measure rates of pay, and the two adjacent measures take inflation into account using closely comparable price indexes. The main conceptual difference is that average hourly earnings measures only part of total pay; it excludes payments by employers on behalf of workers for supplemental benefits such as health plans, social security, and private pension contributions. The gap that opened over time between these measures is attributable to the rise in the share of total pay accounted for by supplemental benefits—from less than 13 percent in 1973 to about 16.5 percent in 1987.

The average worker's total pay, when supplemental benefits are included, has increased during the past 15 years. But the slow rise in output per hour of work has been devoted almost entirely to increased supplementary benefits, leaving little room for an increase in average hourly earnings. Increased payroll tax withheld for social security has also reduced earnings available for consumer spending, and enactment of additional benefit mandates would further widen the gap between total pay and earnings (see Kosters, 1988b).

The Distribution of Wages and Earnings

A second element in the recent controversy about the quality of jobs is what has happened to the distribution of earnings or wages. Conceding that employment growth has been strong during the 1980s, some critics have argued that the shape of the distribution has changed. The basic idea is that although employment growth, mainly in services industries, has included some high-wage professional jobs, these high-wage jobs have been more than offset by disproportionate growth in low-wage jobs. The effects, according to this argument, have been increased polar-ization of wages, shrinkage in the share of middle-class jobs, and a proliferation of low-wage jobs.

The evidence initially put forward in support of this argument in a study released by the Joint Economic Committee in December 1986 was seriously flawed (Bluestone and Harrison, 1986). In addition to its misleading identification of low annual earnings with low wages, the results depended heavily on use of the CPI to take inflation into account, choice of particular years for comparison, and technical features involving selection of a base year and estimation of medians.

In our studies reexamining these data, Murray Ross and I conclude that the shapes of the lower part of earnings distributions have not changed much (Kosters and Ross, 1987a,b; 1988a,b). Moreover, the changes that have occurred cannot be described as disproportionate growth in low-wage jobs, with an increasing proportion of workers slipping below middle-class status. Indeed, for the work force as a whole the proportion of workers with low annual earnings (half the median or less) declined slightly during the past 20 years, with this decline continuing during the 1980s (Figure 2.2). The share of workers in the middle remained about the same, and the share at the upper end increased slightly. These data show a declining share of the work force with low annual earnings. It is important to recognize that the main reason for low annual earnings for these workers was not low wages, but that they only worked part-time or part of the year. In 1985, for example, more than 90 percent of these workers with low annual earnings worked only part-time, part of the year, or both. By examining only year-round, full-time workers, it is possible to reduce to a considerable degree the big differences in annual earnings that are the result of working only a small fraction of the year.

When the same method is applied to year-round, full-time workers the results are different in two important respects. First, the share with low annual earnings (half the median or less) is much smaller—even though their earnings levels are

Percentage

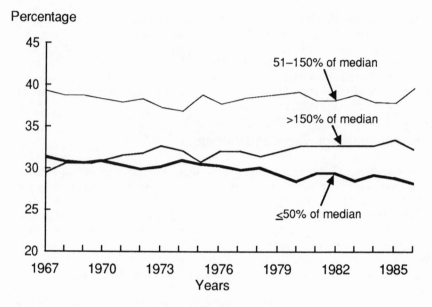

Source: Bureau of the Census *Current Population Survey* Microdata Files

**Figure 2.2   Employment Shares of All Workers by Annual
Earnings Category, 1967–86**

about 50 percent higher. Second, instead of gradually declining over time, the
proportion with low annual earnings first declined from the late 1960s to the late
1970s and then rose again to approximately the same level as in the late 1960s
(Figure 2.3).

The low-earnings proportion of this component of the work force has thus increased since the late 1970s. Since these workers usually worked full-time during
the year and presumably worked (or were on paid leave) for 50 to 52 weeks, annual earnings for this component of the work force correspond more closely to their
wage rates than when all workers with some earnings during the year are analyzed.
Because there is still a great deal of variation in hours of work per week and weeks
of work per year among these workers, it is more illuminating to examine hourly
wages directly to see what has happened to jobs that pay low wages (see Bluestone
and Harrison, 1988; Loveman and Tilly, 1988).

To examine the trend in the proportion of the work force with low hourly wages,
I divided the distribution into three parts. Roughly comparable proportions of the
work force are obtained by defining low wages as 75 percent of the median or less,
high wages as more than 125 percent of the median, and the middle as wages be-

Percentage

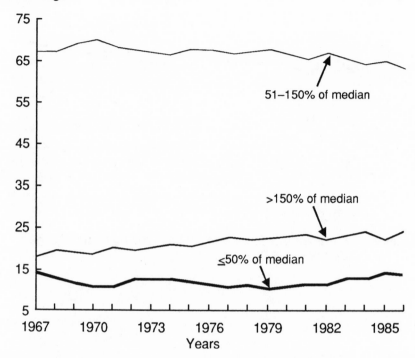

Source: Bureau of the Census *Current Population Survey* Microdata Files

Figure 2.3 Employment Shares of Year-Round Full-Time Workers by Annual Earnings Category, 1967–86

tween those levels. For trends in shares of employment for these hourly wage categories since 1973 see Figure 2.4 for all workers and Figure 2.5 for full-time workers. These data show little overall change in the share with low wages, but the share in the middle declines over time while the high-wage share rises. These data do not support the view that the share of workers with low wages has increased.

The federal minimum wage is a policy element that might be expected to affect low-wage proportions of the work force quite directly. It is generally recognized that the real level of the minimum wage has declined by about 25 percent since 1981. This decline in the minimum wage could be expected to increase the proportion of workers with low wages for two reasons. First, the empirical evidence is quite clear that a lower minimum wage means more jobs than would otherwise

Percentage

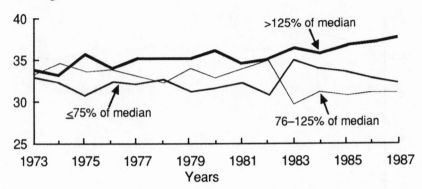

Source: Bureau of the Census *Current Population Survey* Microdata Files

**Figure 2.4   Employment Shares of All Workers by Hourly Wage
Category, 1973–87**

Percentage

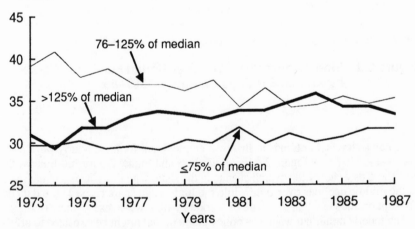

Source: Bureau of the Census *Current Population Survey* Microdata Files

**Figure 2.5   Employment Shares of Full-Time Workers by Hourly
Wage Category, 1973–87**

be created, and most of these additional jobs could be expected to pay relatively low wages at or near the minimum. That is, the additional jobs at low wages might be expected to increase the low-wage proportion of the work force. Second, some of those who would have been employed in the absence of a reduction in the legal minimum would presumably be expected to receive lower wages than if the real level of the minimum had not been reduced. The case for raising the minimum presumably rests entirely on the reasoning underlying this second point. It is, therefore, interesting to examine the effects of the reduction in the real minimum wage on the shape of the overall wage distribution.

The most noteworthy feature of minimum wage effects on the shape of the wage distribution is that, while those in the immediate neighborhood of the minimum wage level are quite pronounced, its effects on the shape of the low end of the wage distribution as a whole are not very apparent. See Figure 2.6 where proportions of full-time and part-time workers below 50 and 75 percent of the median for all workers are charted separately. The federal minimum wage was above 50 percent of the median from 1974 through 1982, but by 1987 the median had risen sufficiently high to bring the 50 percent cutoff well above the minimum.

Consequences for the proportion of workers below 50 percent of the median are strikingly evident for part-time workers, many of whom are teenagers whose main activity is school rather than being a wage earner. The effect is noticeable, but not very pronounced, for full-time workers, and only a very small share of them are employed at low wages. There is essentially no noticeable effect, however, on the proportion of workers earning hourly wages less than 75 percent of the median, even for part-time workers.

So far we have focused on examining segments of the work force below particular earnings or wage rate levels. Another way of examining trends in the shape of the distribution involves computing a measure of dispersion for the distribution as a whole. While it should be recognized that different measures would show somewhat different trends, the coefficient of variation provides a relatively simple measure of percentage variation of wage rates. By this measure, dispersion of hourly wages of workers who are paid by the hour has shown little trend since the early 1970s, for the work force as a whole and for full-time workers (Figure 2.7). Similar measures of dispersion for salaried workers show a pronounced decline over the years, but this may be mainly a result of inflation and fixed nominal dollar limits for reporting high earnings. This combination of circumstances leads to lower measured dispersion in the absence of offsetting adjustments.

In summary, while total hourly pay has risen for the average worker, it has increased more slowly in the past 15 years. Hourly cash wages have been quite stagnant because most of the growth in the total has gone to supplementary benefits.

Evidence on whether wages are less equally distributed is somewhat mixed. There is some sign that the upper end of the distribution has expanded at the expense of the middle. But except in the immediate neighborhood of the minimum wage, the share at the lower end of the distribution seems to have been quite stable.

Employed
Share

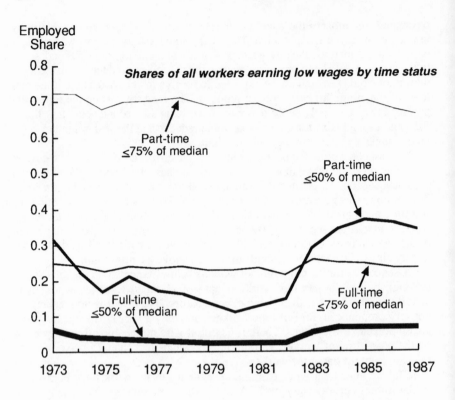

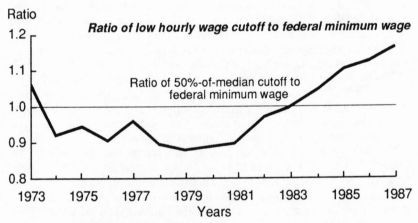

Source: CPS Microdata files

**Figure 2.6   Low-Wage Employment Shares Relative to Federal
Minimum Wage, 1973–87**

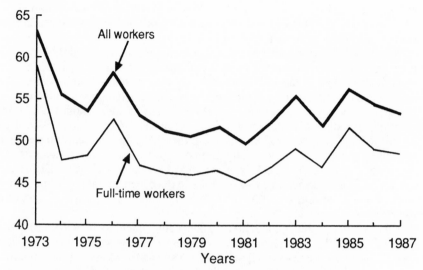

Source: Bureau of the Census *Current Population Survey* Microdata Files

Figure 2.7 Coefficients of Variation for Hourly Wages of Workers Paid by the Hour, 1973–87

Jobs and Industrial Structure

The emergence of the trade deficit in the 1980s gave rise to growing concern about the competitiveness of U.S. manufacturing industries. Increased competition from abroad, especially in the first half of the 1980s, produced pressures for adjustment that included the introduction of new technology to economize on labor costs. One result has been rapid growth in productivity within manufacturing.

Another result of the restructuring taking place in manufacturing, however, is that blue-collar, production worker jobs increasingly account for a small share of new job opportunities. In view of the higher average wages in manufacturing than in industries where employment has been growing more rapidly, such as services, some observers have interpreted the declining share of jobs in manufacturing industries as an indicator of declining average job quality (see Kosters and Ross, 1987b; and for a different interpretation, see Costrell, 1988).

Although the share of real output accounted for by manufacturing industries has been quite stable over the years, the share of total employment in manufacturing has been declining since at least the early 1950s. During the past 20 years, for example, manufacturing employment has varied in a range between 18 and 21 million workers, and it was about in the middle of that range in 1988. Over that same 20-year period, however, total civilian employment increased from about 76 million to 115. This increase of close to 40 million jobs took place almost entirely outside of manufacturing.

The decline in the manufacturing employment share has certainly been pronounced, although it has not been confined to the 1980s. Wages are also higher in manufacturing and, in the absence of changes in distributions within sectors, the decline in the manufacturing share would by itself tend to reduce average wages. But these data only tell part of the story. The rest of the story should at least include the upgrading in occupational categories that has also been taking place. That is, jobs in high-wage occupations, such as professional, managerial, and technical jobs, have grown more rapidly than jobs in occupations with lower wages, skills, and schooling requirements. This upgrading of occupational categories has, by itself, tended to raise average wages; shifts in the occupational mix of jobs have worked in the opposite direction of shifts in the industry employment mix (see McMahon and Tschetter, 1986).

Although blue-collar, production worker employment in manufacturing has declined as a share of total employment, it should be recognized that these jobs have provided only one route to middle-class living standards. Moreover, such production worker jobs provide a route to middle-class (or higher) living levels that is much less well-suited to the interests and qualifications of entering workers than it was a generation ago. Schooling levels have increased greatly for new entrants to the work force compared to those who are retiring from it. Fortunately, adjustments in the labor market have produced job opportunities more closely tailored to the interests and qualifications of young workers, and the contribution of their skills will be invaluable for maintaining competitiveness in world markets and achieving higher living standards.

The difference in schooling levels between recent entrants into the work force and those at retirement age is quite striking. The proportion of workers with fewer than 12 years of schooling is about 12 percent for new entrants compared to about 30 percent for working men near retirement. For women the figures are 7 percent and 22 percent respectively. The proportion of new entrants who have at least completed college is now over 25 percent for both men and women compared to less than 20 percent for men and about 10 percent for women near retirement age. The contrast was even sharper during the 1970s, which may have contributed to lower economic returns to college then.

FAMILY INCOMES

The average family—especially the average middle-class family—is often portrayed as having a hard time making ends meet. Despite important changes in family structure, however, average family income (after adjusting for inflation) reached an all-time high in 1987. After additional adjustment for changes in family size, real family income has increased by 20 percent since 1970 according to data developed by the Congressional Budget Office (CBO, 1988).

The shape of the distribution of income for families has changed over the years. Family income has shown a gradual trend toward a less equal distribution. The trend in the distribution of family income has been influenced by trends in the demographic composition of families. Consequently, changes in the shape of distributions for different types of households have been quite different from those for individual wage earners. For example, although incomes of families (people living with relatives) are less equally distributed than previously, incomes of people not living in families (unrelated individuals) are more equally distributed on the basis of the most commonly cited measures.

Two important demographic trends have contributed to the changing distribution of family incomes. The first is the rising share of families accounted for by single mothers with children, which has tended to increase the share of families at the low end of the distribution. The second is the growing share of husband-wife families with more than one adult member working. This has raised the share at the upper end of the distribution. These two trends have both contributed to a small decline in the proportion of families near the middle of the distribution.

Median adjusted family incomes, as measured in the CBO study mentioned above, have increased over the years for virtually all types of families—elderly and nonelderly, married couples and people living alone, and families with or without children. The one important exception is single mothers. Although it was temporarily higher in the late 1970s, their median income was hardly any higher in 1986 than in 1970. The fraction of these families who fell below the poverty level was essentially unchanged over the entire period, but a large increase in the share of children in poverty occurred because single mothers account for a rising share of all families with children. According to the data reported in the CBO study, single-mother families was the only major household type whose economic status has shown virtually no improvement at the median since 1970, and where there has been a significant deterioration at the lowest and second lowest income quintile levels.

The growing share of single mothers among families with children is one of the most striking changes in the demographic mix of families. From 1970 to 1986 the share of husband-wife families declined from 81 to 71 percent of families with children, while the share accounted for by single-mother families almost doubled from 11 to 20 percent. In 1986 the poverty rate for single-mother families with children was 46 percent compared to 8 percent for husband-wife families. This change in family composition contributes importantly to higher recent poverty rates for families as a whole and for children.

The plight of single mothers is not primarily a problem of low wages for those who are working. Median income for single-mother families declined only for those with no one working. Work experience is evidently a much more important determinant of economic status for such families than their wage level.

Single-mother families include many in which the mother works, and poverty status is influenced importantly by whether she works and how much. For single mothers as a group, two-thirds worked during 1986 and almost 40 percent worked year-round and full-time. For those in poverty, however, about 40 percent worked at some time during the year and only about 8 percent worked year-round and full-time. The poverty rate for those who worked year-round and full-time was 9.4 percent; for those who worked some, 28.3 percent; and for those who did not work at all, 81.7 percent (U.S. Department of Commerce, 1986). These differences associated with work experience are very pronounced and suggest the limitations of policies to raise or supplement wages directly as compared to policies that provide job opportunities in an effort to improve the economic status of this important category of families with children.

The other major development influencing family incomes, versus those of people living alone or with nonrelatives, is the increase in families with more than one earner. Median income of two-earner families is about $40,000—a third higher than families in which only the husband works. The increase in the proportion of families with more than one earner has contributed to a gradual widening of the income distribution for all families. Although the overall share of families with low incomes has not increased over the years, there has been a significant expansion of those in the middle into a higher income range. These trends for family incomes are documented in a detailed study (see Horrigan and Haugen, 1988).

Women in husband-wife families have been forced to work, some have argued, to maintain family living standards. Although whether more wives are working by choice or by necessity is a somewhat subjective judgment, data on incomes of husband-wife families in which the husband is the sole earner are instructive. Real incomes of these families slumped in the mid-1970s and again in the early 1980s (Figure 2.8). The overall income trend for these families is up, however, and by the mid-1980s their incomes exceed those achieved earlier.

Despite their higher average incomes, many families with wives at work may still see themselves as economically squeezed. The income difference surely exaggerates the extent to which they are better off. For one thing, some additional costs are incurred because of work—for transportation, for example, and perhaps for child care—and income tax payments are typically higher. In addition, less time for work at home often means more spending for services. A squeeze attributable to these conditions, however, is quite different from being forced to work to maintain average living standards.

PERFORMANCE AND POLICY

Many of the criticisms of recent trends in the quality of jobs are accompanied by calls for new policies intended to improve performance. The main thrust of these arguments is that policies pursued by the Reagan administration have relied much more extensively on the market with less emphasis on propping up or redistribut-

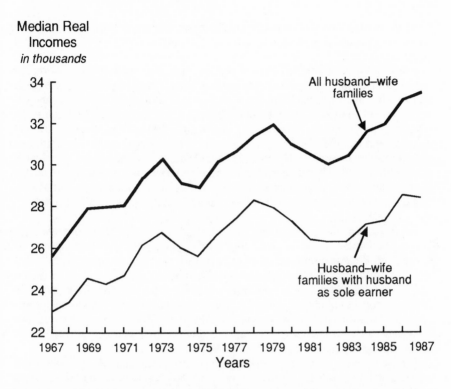

Median Real
Incomes
in thousands

Source: *Labor Force Statistics Derived from the Current Population Survey,* Bureau of Labor Statistics Bulletin no. 2307, Table C-18; values in constant 1986 dollars

Figure 2.8   Median Family Incomes: All Husband-Wife Families and Families with Husband as Sole Earner, 1967–87

ing income. The results, it is argued, are that real wages and living standards declined, poverty increased, and distributions of wages and incomes became less equal. To reverse these trends, it is argued, government should intervene more actively to discourage changes regarded as unfavorable and to foster those thought desirable. Such policies would include protection against employment cutbacks induced by trade competition, restrictions on work force reductions, and an increase in the minimum wage.

It is considerably more difficult to trace differences in performance to changes in policy than to describe actual trends. Since an alleged deterioration in performance has often been ascribed to market-oriented Reagan administration policies, however, it is worthwhile examining appropriate time periods before and during

Reagan's tenure. Although some argue that examining experience before and after 1979 can provide relevant evidence, this is inappropriate from economic and policy perspectives.

From the point of view of the economy, accelerating double-digit inflation during 1979 made the expansion under way then unsustainable by 1980. These conditions were quite different from those that prevailed in 1986 or 1987, years with which recent comparisons have usually been made. From a policy standpoint, the Reagan administration assumed office in 1981, not 1979. And new policies affecting jobs and incomes—such as no further boosts in the minimum wage after the most recent increase in 1981, cutbacks in trade adjustment assistance, elimination of stipends for participants in federal job training programs, and changes in income support program—could be expected to have little effect immediately. Since some critics favor reversal of many of these changes, their effects should be attributed only to the Reagan period.

For a sharper focus on experience under these different policy approaches, it is useful to compare recent data with those for 1977 and 1981, the first years of the Carter and Reagan administrations. The most commonly cited measure of real average hourly earnings, for example, declined by almost 1 percent from 1981 to 1987—but this compares quite favorably with the 8 percent decline from 1977 to 1981. A more comprehensive measure of average wages, adjusted more appropriately for inflation, shows a 4 percent decline by 1981 followed by a 3 percent increase to 1987. And real hourly compensation rose by less than 1 percent before 1981 compared to a 3.3 percent rise by 1987.

Family income changes reflect changes in employment conditions in addition to changes in hourly pay for those employed. Median real income of all households declined by 2 percent from 1977 to 1981 and then rose by 9 percent to 1987. Part of this latter increase might be attributable to more earners in each family. But for husband-wife families with the husband the sole earner, a decline in real income of 3 percent by 1981 was followed by an increase of 7.6 percent by 1987. Similarly, the poverty rate rose from 9.3 percent in 1977 to 11.2 percent in 1981 and declined subsequently to 10.8 percent in 1986.

Of course, economic conditions were different in a variety of ways between these three reference years for comparisons. Nevertheless, these data provide no encouragement to those who argue that retreat from the market-oriented policies of the 1980s would improve performance.

There is considerable merit to the idea of looking at several dimensions of labor market developments. In many instances, of course, whether a trend is desirable is not self-evident, and the interpretation that is placed on particular changes is important. After reviewing the main issues that have been discussed, I conclude that recent performance has on the whole been reasonably good. Although more rapid growth in real wages and incomes would obviously be preferable, there is no evidence of broad deterioration, and most of the evidence points to solid, although not spectacular, improvement.

To the extent that more reliance was placed on the market during the 1980s than previously, or at least more than some critics would prefer, this policy approach has apparently produced constructive results. It facilitated provision of job opportunities for large numbers of new entrants, and it also produced constructive incentives that reward acquisition of work experience and more schooling. The growth of jobs, the changes in the composition of the work force, and the wage flexibility that helped to achieve them also occurred without producing deterioration in average pay or overall distribution of wages and incomes.

EXPERIENCE ABROAD

In addition to examining U.S. experience, it is also useful to consider how this experience compares with experience in other countries. The major European countries in the OECD provide a useful benchmark for comparisons for two reasons. First, OECD-Europe is largely made up of advanced industrial economies that are broadly comparable in many respects to the United States. Second, although most European countries have shifted to some degree toward more reliance on markets, they generally permit less flexibility for response to market forces than in the United States. That is, policy changes in the direction advocated by many critics of the market orientation of U.S. policies would bring U.S. policies more closely in line with those that have prevailed in OECD-Europe (see Kosters, 1986).

The most fundamental point to make with regard to comparisons of U.S. experience with that in other countries is that the slowdown in productivity growth has been a worldwide phenomenon. Although productivity growth during the 1960s and early 1970s was higher in OECD-Europe than in the United States—and much higher in Japan—the rate of growth for broadly comparable measures of productivity growth slowed down a great deal in each case (Table 2.1). Moreover, productivity growth in the United States has recovered to about 1 percent per year in the 1980s after showing no increase from 1973 to 1979. Japan and OECD-Europe, in contrast, experienced about the same growth in productivity during most of the 1970s as in the 1980s.

Although productivity growth has been slower for all countries since 1973, in OECD-Europe it has remained higher than in the United States. This higher productivity growth has been accompanied by some growth in real wages in the European economies. But employment in Europe has been stagnant in contrast to strong employment growth in the United States. The result has been much higher unemployment rates in Europe by the mid-1980s than in the United States, a dramatic reversal of comparative experience during the 1960s and 1970s.

These different circumstances have sometimes been characterized in the following manner. Europe has followed a high-wage strategy, with less emphasis on job creation than in this country. The United States, in contrast, has emphasized strong employment growth, but the result has been wage stagnation. Stating the compari-

Table 2.1   Basic Economic Comparisons—United States, Japan, and European OECD Members, 1960–85

Measure	Annual Percentage Change			
	1960–73	73–79	79–85	73–85
Productivity Growth (GDP/person employed)				
United States	2.0	0.0	1.1	0.5
Japan	8.2	2.9	3.0	2.9
OECD-Europe	4.3	2.1	1.5	1.8
Employment Growth				
United States	1.9	2.5	1.4	2.0
Japan	1.3	0.7	1.0	0.8
OECD-Europe	0.4	0.3	-0.1	0.1
Real Hourly Wage Growth (manufacturing)				
United States	1.4	0.0	-0.7	-0.3
Japan	7.0	1.6	1.4	1.5
OECD-Europe	N.A.	2.8	1.1	2.0
Growth in GDP per Capita				
United States	2.7	1.4	1.4	1.4
Japan	8.3	2.5	3.3	2.9
OECD-Europe	3.8	1.9	0.9	1.4
Population Growth				
United States	1.2	1.0	1.0	1.0
Japan	1.1	1.1	0.7	0.9
OECD-Europe	1.0	0.5	0.5	0.5

	1973	1979	1985
Unemployment Rates (percentage of total labor force)			
United States	4.7	5.8	7.1
Japan	1.3	2.1	2.6
OECD-Europe	3.6	6.2	11.0

Source: OECD-Europe Economic Outlook, Historical Statistics, 1987.

Notes: Real wages for the United States were calculated by dividing the wage index by the CPI. GDP is gross domestic product. The pattern of unemployment rates has remained essentially unchanged from 1986 to 1988.

son in these terms may suggest that which strategy is preferable is an open question, so it is illuminating to carry the analysis a step farther.

Questions that should be considered include: Which strategy has resulted in higher growth in output per capita? Or under which strategy has per capita output growth held up better? Per capita output growth in the United States since 1973 compares quite favorably with that in OECD-Europe (Table 2.1). Moreover, the slowdown in U.S. per capita output growth has been much smaller than in OECD-Europe.

Note that these comparisons are not a result of higher population growth in Europe. On the contrary, population growth in Europe has not only been slower than in the United States, it has also slowed down more sharply since 1973. When these differential population growth rates are taken into account, the comparison of growth in output per capita is even more favorable for the United States.

In summary, these comparisons do not suggest that policies that buttress wage levels or blunt incentives for labor market adjustment in Europe have produced more favorable results. Instead, output per capita has not increased more rapidly in the European economies despite their slower population growth. In addition, slow employment growth in Europe has produced extraordinarily high unemployment, deprived many workers of valuable work experience, and left these economies plagued by serious long-term unemployment problems. It is difficult to find encouragement in these comparisons for policies that would place less reliance on the market forces that foster adjustment and promote jobs and employment growth.

THE LABOR MARKET OUTLOOK

The influence of some factors that affect the outlook for jobs and wages in the decade ahead will be felt more or less independently of the policy environment. Demographic change is an example. The outlook could also be influenced by policy changes intended either to affect jobs, wages, or working conditions directly or to contribute to other goals. My discussion of the outlook first addresses some policy questions and then turns to other features of the outlook.

The likely trend for labor productivity growth is without doubt the most important element in the outlook for jobs and living standards. Productivity growth is the underlying source of increases in real earnings and living standards. It determines how well the typical worker fares. It has also historically been the primary determinant of how workers at the low end of the income distribution have fared and of the poverty rate. Growth in real wages and earnings for the distribution as a whole has been far more important for the typical worker and for those with relatively low income than changes in the shapes of distributions.

Unfortunately, from the point of view of assessing the outlook, our ability to predict the future growth of productivity is very limited, as is our understanding of how policy changes might affect productivity growth. Investment in physical capital has made a small, but important, contribution in the past. Human capital investment—basic schooling and development of sophisticated technical skills—has also been important. Development of new technology and improvement of our knowledge base have probably been at least as important.

What general prescriptions for policy can be drawn from what we know about the sources of productivity growth? First, a favorable climate for investment—in order of their importance, perhaps, for human capital, research and development, and physical capital—is an important general prescription. Fostering conditions that lead to efficient use of available resources is another, and extensive reliance on prices and markets is most likely to foster these conditions.

The two areas where policy may pose the most significant threats to improved productivity and living standards are international trade and preferential treatment for particular industries or employment and pay practices. Trade deficits that are likely to continue to be uncomfortably large—despite some limited progress in reducing our federal budget deficit and a probable rise in private savings to more normal rates—will intensify political pressures to intervene directly in efforts to reduce bilateral imbalances between countries and for particular industry sectors. Even though pursuing such policies would probably influence the composition of trade flows more than the net balance, higher prices to consumers would tend to reduce living standards, and smaller capital inflows—if achieved—might reduce investment.

Pressures for preferential treatment for particular industries might arise from efforts to save jobs or maintain production in contexts as varied as environmental policy, trade policy, or development of new technology. Our experience with a wide range of such policies is not promising, either in terms of returns to the investment that is encouraged or in terms of effects on worker productivity.

The limited scope for new federal spending programs in view of continuing federal budget deficits has already stimulated political interest in alternative ways of furthering the interests of constituencies. These alternatives range from notification requirements for major layoffs and plant closings to proposals for a higher minimum wage, mandatory health plan coverage, and child care and parental leave requirements. The common feature of many of these proposals is that, although they appear to provide benefits to workers at employers' expense, their practical effect is to place employers in the position of providing particular nonwage benefits in exchange for lower cash wages instead of relying on taxing and spending by government. Unless employers can provide such benefits particularly efficiently and allocate them to workers who value them most, such programs will reduce instead of improve living standards.

Changes in the demographic composition of the work force are in prospect irrespective of policy. Some of these changes will tend to raise average real wages, others will tend to reduce them. Overall, the effects during the decade are likely to be positive for real wages and even more so for living standards.

The main factors expected to contribute to higher average real wages are the more favorable schooling and experience composition of the work force. Absorption of the baby boom generation into the work force has led to a work force with relatively little work experience. The wage premium for more schooling and work experience has increased significantly, and real wages should reflect the returns to investments of both kinds that have been made during the past two decades.

The prospect of a continuing rise in the labor force participation of women will give rise to two quite different effects. Despite strong gains in wages and earnings for women relative to men in the 1980s, their average wages are still well below those of men. The compositional effects of more women in the work force will, consequently, tend to dilute increases in the overall average even though women's relative wages can be expected to continue rising. On the other hand, a higher proportion of the populace at work will mean higher per capita income, and higher family income as well unless offsetting changes take place in family structure.

Prospective changes in the work force also have important implications for employers. The trough in birth rates that followed the baby boom means that the number of young workers entering the work force during the 1990s will be far smaller than during the mid-1960s to the mid-1980s. Employers will find young and inexperienced workers who are willing to work for relatively low wages in much shorter supply.

Changing conditions in the labor market, however, have also opened new opportunities and challenges for employers. The decline in relative wages for young workers and workers with low levels of schooling means that employers would be well-advised to consider hiring these classes of workers if they are able to train them to fulfill their job requirements and retain them for a sufficient period to recoup their investment. Employers who are able to adapt to these emerging labor market conditions will profit by developing the necessary training and job development programs. The demographic categories who will benefit from the combination of tight labor market and better work experience and on-the-job training opportunities are those who have fared least well during the past two decades.

Note

1. David Henderson, head of the Economics and Statistics Department of the Organization for Economic Cooperation and Development (OECD), describes this policy emphasis in an undated paper, portraying the emphasis on markets and deregulation as characteristic of a wide range of Western countries.

References

Bluestone, Barry and Bennett Harrison (1986) "The Great American Job Machine: The Proliferation of Low Wage Employment in the U.S. Economy." A Study Prepared for the Joint Economic Committee, The Congress of the United States. Boston: University of Massachusetts/Boston.

Bluestone, Barry and Bennett Harrison (1988) "The Growth of Low-Wage Employment: 1963–86." *The American Economic Review* 78(2):124–28.

Congressional Budget Office (1988) *Trends in Family Income: 1970–1986.* Washington, DC: Congressonal Budget Office, The Congress of the United States.

Costrell, Robert M. (1988). *The Effects of Industry Employment Shifts on Wage Growth: 1948–87. A Study Prepared for the Use of the Joint Economic Committee, Congress of the United States.* Washington, DC: U.S. Government Printing Office.

Henderson, David (n.d.) "Perestroika in the West: Progress, Limits, and Implications." Paris: Economics and Statistics Department, the Organization for Economic Cooperation and Development.

Horrigan, Michael W. and Steven E. Haugen (1988) "The Declining Middle-Class Thesis: A Sensitivity Analysis." *Monthly Labor Review* 111(5):3–13.

Kosters, Marvin H. (1986) "On Economic Flexibility: Free Markets Bring Change and Growth." *Challenge* 29(1):55–64.

Kosters, Marvin H. (1988a) "Jobs and Pay—A Review of Recent Performance." *The AEI Economist* [American Enterprise Institute] November.

Kosters, Marvin H. (1988b). "Mandated Benefits—On the Agenda." *Regulation. AEI Journal on Government and Society* [American Enterprise Institute] no. 3:21–27.

Kosters, Marvin H. and Murray N. Ross (1987a) "The Distribution of Earnings and Employment Opportunities: A Re-examination of the Evidence." American Enterprise Institute Occasional Paper. Washington, DC: American Enterprise Institute.

Kosters, Marvin H. and Murray N. Ross (1987b) "The Influence of Employment Shifts and New Job Opportunities on the Growth and Distribution of Real Wages." *Deficits, Taxes, and Economic Adjustments,* edited by Phillip Cagan, 209–42. Contemporary Economic Problems. Washington, DC: American Enterprise Institute.

Kosters, Marvin H. and Murray N. Ross (1988a) "The Quality of Jobs: Evidence from Distributions of Annual Earnings and Hourly Wages." American Enterprise Institute Occasional Paper. Washington, DC: American Enterprise Institute.

Kosters, Marvin H. and Murray N. Ross (1988b) "A Shrinking Middle Class?" *The Public Interest* no. 90:3–27.

Loveman, Gary W. and Chris Tilly (1988) "Good Jobs or Bad Jobs: What Does the Evidence Say?" *New England Economic Review Federal Reserve Bank of Boston* (January/February):46–65.

McMahon, Patrick J. and John H. Tschetter (1986) "The Declining Middle Class: A Further Analysis." *Monthly Labor Review* 109(9):22–27.

Monthly Labor Review Staff (1985) "The Effect of Rental Equivalence on the Consumer Price Index, 1967–82." *Monthly Labor Review* 108(3):3–10.

U.S. Department of Commerce, Bureau of the Census (1986) *Poverty in the United States.* Current Population Reports, Series P-60, *Consumer Income,* no. 160.

COMMENT

David E. Bloom

Marvin Kosters' main message is that free-market policies pursued under the Reagan administration strengthened the U.S. economy "without producing deterioration in average pay or in the overall distribution of wages and income." He also projects an image of the U.S. labor market in the future, although this is of secondary interest judging from the amount of space Kosters devotes to this issue. I discuss these two aspects of Kosters' chapter in reverse order.

Kosters' discussion of the labor market outlook is interesting, although not as deep or far-reaching as it could be. Kosters first tells us that "the likely trend for labor productivity growth is without doubt the most important element in the outlook for jobs and living standards." But in the next breath he asserts that "our ability to predict the future growth of productivity is very limited." Kosters then observes that the present demographic structure of the United States implies increasingly tight labor markets that will result in upward pressure on real wages. Although this is not an original insight, there is considerable sense in this observation. But there is a hitch in Kosters' follow-through on this point because he overlooks the many important adaptations that will naturally take place in response to tight labor markets.

In reviewing recent labor market history in the United States, Kosters tries to straighten us out regarding recent trends in average pay and income inequality (whether average real pay has increased or decreased, and whether its distribution has become more or less unequal). He reads the facts as indicating that "the average worker's total pay . . . has increased during the past 15 years" and that "the shapes of earnings distributions have not changed much." He interprets the facts "as consistent with the view that more market-oriented policies have contributed to better [economic] performance instead of detracting from it."

With regard to his discussion of recent trends in earnings and inequality, Kosters feels that "what has actually occurred has sometimes been misunderstood." Having read much of the literature in this area, including the chapter by Barry Bluestone, my view on this matter is even more dubious: what has actually occurred is not yet fully known!

Differences of opinion over the facts themselves are in most cases the result of different judgments made about the most sensible way to look at available data: Should we focus on household income, family income, or individual income? Or should we examine earnings instead? Should the earnings be annual, weekly, or hourly? Over what time period should we make comparisons? How shall we account for inflation and business cycle fluctuations in making those comparisons? What measures of income inequality should we calculate? Unfortunately, this substantive area is one in which the conclusions one draws are highly sensitive to the empirical strategy one adopts. Consumers of this genre of literature on inequality should beware of the ease with which analysts can conjure up evidence that suits their ideological preconceptions.

Although Kosters rightly argues for care in empirical analysis, his chapter brings to mind the image of a man in a glass house throwing stones. Kosters fails to report inequality measures separately for members of different demographic groups, although most other analyses in this area, including his earlier work with Ross, reveal differential trends for men (increasing inequality) and women (declining inequality). That these trends tend to cancel each other out in Kosters' combined data does not absolve him of explaining the trends that are so readily apparent in the analysis of disaggregated data. Kosters also ignores completely what is perhaps the most striking change in the structure of wages in the United States since the Great Depression: the widening wage gap across educational classes that has occurred among men during the 1980s. Increased earnings inequality among men is presumably closely related to the rising educational premium.

As noted earlier, Kosters argues that market-oriented policies established during the Reagan administration promoted U.S. economic performance. This conclusion is based on two types of "thought experiments": a comparison of labor market performance (1) before and during the Reagan administration and (2) in the United States and Western Europe. The experiences of the United States in the 1970s and Western Europe in the 1980s are treated as "controls" in the experiments, examples of economies with policies that constrained the operation of market forces. Although Kosters' basic approach to this issue has merit, neither of these experiments is conclusive.

Comparing the 1970s to the 1980s, Kosters makes little attempt to "partial out" the effects of many other variables unrelated to market freedom that changed during the 1980s. Barry Bluestone discusses many of these changes. Other papers not cited by Kosters have documented the contribution of two specific developments during the 1980s to increased earnings inequality among white men: the fall in the real value of the minimum wage and the decline of unionism. Kosters' assertions to the contrary notwithstanding, both of these developments are at least arguably related to Reagan administration policies.

Regarding his comparison of the experiences of Western Europe and the United States, Kosters infers too much. There is little rigor in a line of thought that basically says the United States is market-oriented, Western Europe is not, the United States did better, and therefore market-oriented policy is better than intervention. In addition, it is not obvious that the types of intervention Kosters specifically criticizes—plant closing notifications, restrictions on employment reductions, and worker retraining—will have a significant impact on *national* labor market data.

Finally, treating Western Europe as a monolith from the standpoint of economic policy and performance is far from satisfactory; it also overlooks the much richer thought experiment implicit in the cross-country comparisons that can be made within Western Europe.

The irony in all of this is that Kosters' conclusions may in fact be correct. But as his chapter now stands, they are little more than speculations not strongly founded in hard economic research.

My last comment concerns the absence in this chapter (and in Barry Bluestone's as well) of any discussion of the "ideal" income distribution. Logically speaking, it makes little sense to bemoan or applaud any trend in inequality without first defining—and justifying—the target at which one is aiming. We would be better off if Kosters, Bluestone, and other students of income distribution redirected some of their intellectual energy away from disputing a set of relatively pedestrian measurement issues and toward thinking more deeply about the reasons underlying our interest in those issues.

3 SOURCES OF JOB GROWTH —AND SOME IMPLICATIONS

David L. Birch

Our research group at MIT—The Program on Jobs, Entrepreneurs, and Markets—began to study the economy of the United States by breaking it down into the individual pieces from which it is built—the individual business establishments. We followed each one over a 20-year period, and then added them all back up. When we were finished, we had studied the histories of over 17 million individual business addresses that today employ approximately 95 percent of our private-sector work force.

When we looked through this "economic microscope," the first thing we noticed was enormous churning and turbulence. As a nation we are losing 7 or 8 percent of our jobs and companies every year. We have to replace about 50 percent of our job base every five years just to break even.

This degree of turbulence offers great opportunity for change, and change is certainly occurring. We initially saw the change as a structural shift from manufacturing services. Superficially it looks that way. We have created about 40 million jobs since 1968, and not one of them is in manufacturing. We have fewer manufacturing jobs today than we had 20 years ago. We are down to the point where only about 8 percent of our work force actually goes to work in a factory every day.

A more accurate description of change, though, is a shift to higher and higher rates of innovation. Companies and places that are growing are the ones that innovate a great deal.

Much of the innovation is occurring in the more mature manufacturing sectors. Two manufacturing economies, one old and one new, coexist side by side. We find high rates of innovation and rapid growth in young companies beside declining older companies in the same industry. We find it in steel, in textiles, in clothing, in bicycles, in paper, and so forth. In fact, if all industries in the United States are ranked by the percentage of their companies that are growing rapidly,

30 of the top 40 ranked industries are in manufacturing, and all manufacturing sectors are above the national average on this measure.

Some of the innovation is taking place in the actual inventing and making of new technology—the so-called high-technology segment. But high tech is a very small part of our economy, around 3 or 4 percent. More important, its growth is slowing down in the face of automation and overseas competition. By my estimate, it will amount to only 4 or 5 percent of all jobs 10 years from now, and will account for at most 5 percent of the job growth in the next 10 years. It is not nearly so important as most people think.

Most of the net growth in our economy comes from innovation arising out of the application of technology to create new services that have no hardware product. These innovations can be found in a great diversity of industries, ranging from software to finance, education, telecommunications, consulting, health care, insurance, distribution, hospital management, even trash collection.

SOURCES OF JOB GROWTH

This "Innovation Revolution" is affecting the structure of our corporate world. There are tremendous opportunities for innovation and corporate formation in what I call the "thoughtware sectors." These sectors are experiencing high innovation rates and rapid corporate formation and growth. The barriers to entry are, in general, very low and the formation rates have been growing steadily. In 1950, around 90 thousand new firms were started in the United States. By 1965, the number was 200 thousand; by 1975 it was 300 thousand; by 1981 it was around 600 thousand; today it is over 700 thousand. These numbers do not include partnerships and newly self-employed people. Partnerships add another 100 thousand new enterprises a year; the newly self-employed have been averaging 500 thousand in recent years. In sum, we are now starting about 1.3 million enterprises per year.

This trend is beginning to have a significant effect on the sources of employment growth. In our initial research covering 1969 to 1976, we found that firms with 20 or fewer employees created about two-thirds of all new jobs, and that firms with under 100 employees created about 80 percent of the new jobs. Since then, many groups have looked at many periods for the nation and for individual states. It is safe to conclude at this point, first, that smaller firms are virtually always disproportionately large creators of jobs. Their share of job creation is almost always greater than their share of jobs in the economy. Second, the small business share of job creation varies greatly from one period to the next and from one place to the next. There is no magic number describing smaller business's role. Third, we know that most variation in the small business share of job creation is attributable to the erratic performance of large firms. Small businesses are fairly steady job creators from one year to the next. Large firms, on the other hand, have good periods such as 1976–80 and 1984–87, and bad periods like 1974–75 and 1980–83. As a consequence of the erratic performance of large firms, the small business share can vary anywhere from 40 percent to over 100 percent (when large firms collectively decline). Fourth, we have learned that small firms are particularly important during recession. During recessions when large firms collectively slow down, small firms serve as a kind of inertia wheel.

Looking at the period from 1980 to 1988 on a cruder scale, the nation created approximately 17.5 million jobs. During that same interval, the Fortune 500 have eliminated 3.5 million employees. The Fortune 500 losses are substantially greater than the entire work force, public and private, of the State of Massachusetts. Last year alone, the United States added 3.6 million jobs to its economy, and the Fortune 500 eliminated 400 thousand employees. In 1980, the Fortune 500 employed 77 percent of all manufacturing workers; today they employ only 65 percent. In contrast, the non-Fortune 500, who employed only 23 percent in 1980, are now up to 35 percent. We have reached the point where only about 5 percent of the work force goes to work in a Fortune 500 factory every day.

An analysis of the individual Fortune 500 companies reveals an increasingly volatile and vulnerable collection of firms. In the first quarter century of the Fortune 500 (1955–80) only about 48 percent of the 500 turned over—that is, about 48 percent of the firms were replaced and 52 percent remained the same. In the 11 years from 1970 to 1981, 33 percent turned over, and during the last 5 years alone, 30 percent were replaced. Said another way, in the 1960s it took approximately 20 years for a third of the Fortune 500 to be replaced. In the 1970s it took only 10 years to accomplish the same thing, and in the 1980s it has taken only 5 years. According to our statistics, today a small company is only twice as likely to vanish as a Fortune 500 company in any five-year period. In fact, a job in a small firm is now more secure than one in a Fortune 500 company.

A great concern with this reordering of the manufacturing economy is its effect on the balance of payments because, it is suggested, small firms do not export. We have looked at 40 thousand United States exporters recently and discovered that, contrary to popular belief, a small firm with 50 to 99 employees is now more likely to export than a company with over 500 employees.

The phenomenon of small business growth is not evenly distributed across companies. It is useful to think of firms in terms of three groups. I like to call them elephants, gazelles, and mice. Elephants are the seven thousand large, publicly-traded companies in the United States. Mice are the seven million small firms that start, reach their initial employment within a few months, and stay at that size for the rest of their corporate lives. Gazelles are the 700 thousand firms that are growing at 20 percent per year or more in any given five-year period.

We've just looked at the recent experience of elephants. The mice are important primarily because they keep starting. Assuming that each of the 1.3 million new enterprises formed each year employs only two people, that amounts to 2.6 million jobs, or almost 70 percent of all new jobs formed in the United States.

The gazelles are important primarily because of their growth. Their purpose when formed is to grow. While they account for only 5 to 10 percent of the firms, they account for almost 80 or 90 percent of the net job creation among existing firms in any given interval. In fact, looking at the set of firms that existed in 1983 and 1988, we find the top 5 percent created 87 percent of all new jobs created by that group, and the top 10 percent accounted for 96 percent of the new jobs. If the next five years is anything like the last five, 86 percent of the gazelles today employ 20 or fewer people, and 98 percent employ 100 or fewer people. Gazelles are highly volatile. In fact, the single best predictor of growth in the gazelle population is previous decline, the single best predictor of decline is previous growth, and the single best predictor of death is stability.

SOME IMPLICATIONS

There are many interesting implications of the phenomena just described for places. First, we know that the loss rates of jobs are remarkably similar everywhere. Most places in the United States lose 7 or 8 percent of their jobs—plus or minus 1 or 2 percent—every year. We know also that migration is relatively insignificant. Very few firms move from one place to another, and those who do account for no more than three- or four-tenths of 1 percent of the job change in any given area.

The net gain in employment in a location is thus almost entirely because of the rate at which jobs are replaced, and most of the replacement is attributable to firms starting and firms growing. We know that the replacement rate varies enormously from one place to another—by a factor of 8 or 10.

What is the cause of this great variation in replacement rate? In the old days it was inexpensive land and labor, low-cost energy, harbors and rail lines, and so on. In the "new economy," as I call it, the fastest growing places are now the ones with the highest costs. The issue is no longer cost, it is quality. Gazelles are attracted to major university research centers. The best example I know of is in my backyard—East Cambridge, Massachusetts. From 1980 to 1988, the two-thirds of a square mile constituting East Cambridge created more jobs than six states in the United States. Gazelles are attracted to a skilled labor force. They are attracted to airports, preferably hubs, so that they can reach their many customers and suppliers quickly. They are attracted to a high quality of life. They are attracted to a place that offers an attractive entrepreneurial climate. The entrepreneurial climate is difficult to measure directly, but we see considerable variation in the ability and willingness of entrepreneurs to start and grow from one place to another.

Looking below the metropolitan area level at 619 subareas within metropolitan areas, we find a very strong pattern of what Joel Garreau of the *Washington Post* calls "edge cities." These cities are places like Marietta and Roswell near Atlanta, Georgia; Plano and Richardson in the Dallas area of Texas; Herndon and Manassas, Virginia, outside Washington, DC; Princeton and New Brunswick, New Jersey, near New York; and Santa Ana and Costa Mesa, California, outside Los Angeles. There are very few such places. A large area like Los Angeles or New York or Chicago might have only two or three, and most cities have only one. These places are characterized by their distance from the central city, which tends to be on the order of 10 to 20 miles. They tend to be near airports, occupying relatively inexpensive land, and they are almost uniformly as far away from poor people and black people as possible.

RESEARCH PRIORITIES AND CONCLUSION

Given the state of our knowledge, I see four top priorities for research related to job creation in the future. The first is to examine the issues surrounding data bases. All microdata bases (public and private) used to study the processes by which jobs are created have gaping holes in them. We need to consolidate what we know about the nature of the holes, and how best to compensate for them. This is a particularly opportune time to address data base issues, since the unemployment insurance system is being thoroughly investigated on the public side, and Dun and Bradstreet and other private sources are enhancing their own data bases significantly.

My second priority would be to study the process by which corporations evolve. We know that corporations do not follow life cycles like human beings do. They do not grow, mature, stabilize, and decline. They are volatile throughout their life. They grow at different ages; in fact, the greatest growth age is 75 years or older. Firms start slowly, not rapidly, when they are young. They die at all ages, and in fact more die at a young age than at an old age. We know these facts, but we do not really understand the growth process in detail as a whole. We do not understand what stimulates it. We do not understand what paths it follows with any accuracy. And we do not understand what stops it.

My third priority is to understand the work force implications of job creation. First we need to understand what it means for the individual. Individuals in the system I have just described experience very high mobility. One person in five changes jobs every year. One in 10 is forced to change jobs every year. And almost one in 10 changes careers every year. There is very little job security today, particularly in large companies. In addition, there is a great need for new skills. The old jobs are not like the new ones. In fact, there is a great mismatch between current skills and the needs of newly created jobs.

Also, there are implications for special groups within the population. There is a strong spatial dimension to what is happening. Boomtowns are being built at the edge of cities. In the face of a work force shortage, we are creating jobs as far away from our surplus labor pools as possible. This situation represents a second major mismatch. We must come to grips with it. We can move people, or jobs, or both, but something has to give.

My fourth priority relates to international variations. It is trite to say today that the world economy is more interdependent and that we are being affected adversely by it. But it is important to go beneath that generalization and see what it means for individual companies in the United States and abroad. We have found, for example, that smaller companies are now more likely to export than larger ones. How do we encourage more of that? What does it all mean in detail for different economies as a whole? We tend to talk of the Western countries as though they were pretty much the same. I have studied the United Kingdom, Canada, and Sweden in detail. There are some common threads, particularly the propensity for larger companies to be declining everywhere, including Japan. But there are some great differences. There is great variation in the degree of turbulence. There is great variation in the degree of entrepreneurship and corporate ownership. Understanding these variations in detail will tell us a great deal about how to increase trade, who to increase it with, and what to trade.

These are my top priorities. I think we have barely scratched the surface in understanding the processes by which jobs are created, and how individuals and communities relate to that process. The stakes are quite high. We no longer have a surplus labor pool. Virtually all of our growth and prosperity will depend on our ability to connect jobs and people in a far more effective manner. It is thus entirely appropriate that we reflect on research and develop informed policies that address this key problem.

4 FOREIGN INVESTMENT AND AMERICAN JOBS

Norman J. Glickman and Douglas P. Woodward

Across this country, foreign companies have been acquiring existing businesses and starting new ones. Between 1980 and 1987, multinational corporations like Mitsubishi, Seagrams, Siemens, and Philips have quadrupled their ownership of American industry. They make everything from cars to clothing and sell everything from insurance to zippers. They refine oil, operate vineyards, lend money, and write advertising copy. Carnation, Mack Trucks, Brooks Brothers, Smith and Wesson, *Ms.* magazine, and Pillsbury are familiar "American" brand names owned by foreign investors. Foreigners have cut huge real estate deals and now own such major buildings as the ABC Building and ARCO Plaza. Ted Bates (advertising), CS First Boston (finance), Bloomingdales (clothing), and Hardees (food retailing) are examples of foreign-owned firms in the fast-growing service sector. The list is long, the industries diverse. Moreover, with this wave of investment carries new management practices, labor relations, and technology. Not only do foreign firms control more of the American economy, but they have become actively involved in politics, culture, philanthropy, and other aspects of community life.

THE GROWING DEBATE OVER FOREIGN INVESTMENT

Such investment has begun to change the way we live and work, although we may not be always aware of its influence. An American can buy Chicken-of-the-Sea Tuna (owned by an Indonesian company) from A&P (West Germany) or dresses from Bonwit Teller (Canada) with a credit card from Marine Midland Bank (Hong Kong). She may drive a Plymouth Laser (Japan), read a Doubleday book (West Germany), swig a Lone Star beer (Australia), and listen to Willie Nelson on CBS Records (Japan). Basic Books has published our book on foreign investment, *The New Competitors* (Glickman and Woodward, 1989). Basic is a subsidiary of the Australian-based News Incorporated, owned by Rupert Murdoch.

77

Until recently, most people were unlikely to know that they were dealing with foreign companies operating in this country. Many probably did not care. Yet suddenly there is an American fixation with what we call the "new competitors," foreign companies that have acquired U.S. companies or built new plants or offices here. With so many companies under foreign control, it is not hard to understand why the public has concerns. A 1988 public opinion poll showed 74 percent of Americans believing that foreign investment means that America has less control over the economy. Fully 78 percent were in favor of a law limiting foreign investment in business and real estate (*Business Week* Staff, 1984). But foreign investors raise hope as well as suspicion. Many Americans see foreign direct investment as the savior of American industry and jobs, pointing to the doubling in the number of Americans working for foreigners in the last 15 years.

Often conflicting public policy questions have come with this surge of investment. We focus on two here. Has increased foreign investment meant giving up a large proportion of our assets and with it control of our economy? And, does foreign direct investment revitalize the economy by creating jobs?

Foreign Investment and Jobs

On the jobs issue, many news reports have highlighted the reindustrialization potential (that is, the ability to provide new jobs, especially in manufacturing) of foreign investment, arguing that such investment promises to be one of the most important economic forces reshaping America as the century concludes. For example, a *Business Week* report suggests that the Japanese are reshaping our cities and regions:

> A new wave of Japanese investment is sweeping across America. Unlike earlier commitments to coastal areas, this second wave is reaching deep into the heartland. It is spawning Japanese industrial centers such as "Auto Alley," stretching into the mid-South and "Silicon Forest" in the Northwest. It is giving failing American companies a fresh start through infusions of capital and management. And it is providing new sources of financing to local and state governments, which were once suspicious and fearful of outsiders. (*New York Times* Staff, 1985:33)

What *Business Week* wrote about Japan others said about the investments by multinational corporations (MNCs) of other nations, particularly those based in the United Kingdom, Canada, West Germany, and the Netherlands.

There is no question that many federal government officials stand squarely in favor of these trends. The conventional wisdom in Washington is that any move to restrict foreign investment would be counterproductive. Washington's open door attitude is mild, however, compared with the active policy adopted by many states and cities. To state and local officials anxious to attract new sources of jobs and tax revenues, foreign multinational corporations are honored guests, eagerly recruited and favorably received. To many, foreign investment holds out hope for industrial rejuvenation. Kentucky ponied up more than $300 million in subsidies to corral a Toyota plant, for example. As the responsibility for economic development has fallen to state and local policymakers, it may turn the attention to foreign capital. Georgia's Governor Joe Harris claims that foreign companies in his state are "replacing jobs that have been lost from American manufacturing operations . . . " (*New York Times* Staff, 1985:D9).

Foreign Investment, Foreign Control

However, some observers are beginning to question the wisdom of global smokestack chasing. To them, the surge in foreign ownership does not signify the dawn of an industrial renaissance, but a surrender of our productive resources to foreign control. Perhaps, they say, future economic historians will look upon the period since the mid-1970s as a watershed—marking the onset of a de-Americanized economy, a time when we lost our economic independence. This jingoistic theme is personified by June Collier, the CEO of National Industries, Inc., who has "nightmares" about U.S. business becoming subsidiaries of Japan, Saudi Arabia, or France. She founded Citizens Against Foreign Control of America (CAFCA) "to find out the truth about foreign control." She argues that foreigners find it "cheaper to buy us than to bomb us" (Collier, 1988:10A).

Few Americans have such "CAFCA-esque" nightmares about foreigners. However, even the thoughtful observers, such as Wall Street financier Felix Rohatyn (1988), whose firm has represented foreign and domestic firms in foreign buyouts, said, "the United States has lost its status as an independent power" and talked about the possibility of putting controls on foreign investment. Malcolm Forbes (1988:17), a noted free marketeer, called for a strict review of "*any* foreign purchase of *any* significance . . . of *any* consequential U.S. company—regardless of size." The Congressional debate over the 1988 trade bill also involved discussions of greater restrictions on and disclosure of foreign direct investment.

ESSENTIAL FACTS ABOUT FOREIGN INVESTMENT

Some of the divergence of views over foreign investment results from gross misunderstandings about it, in part because government data do not allow us a full analysis of foreign direct investment in the United States (FDIUS).[1] Despite the lack of important information, it is possible to get at some important points about FDIUS. Here are some essential facts to remember:

● FDIUS comes from the world's most advanced industrial countries—especially the United Kingdom, Continental Europe, Canada, and Japan. A popular misconception is that a FDIU is a "Japanese phenomenon." It is not. Although, Japanese investment is growing fastest, it is still third behind Britain and the Netherlands (Figure 4.1).

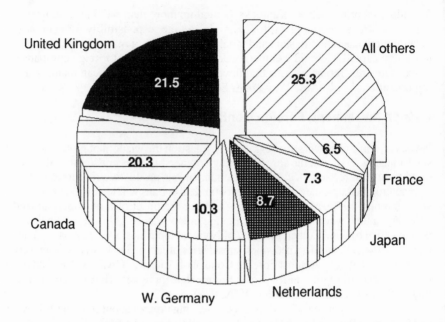

Source: Survey of Current Business, May 1988

**Figure 4.1   Who Invests in America?   Percentage of Employment
by Foreigners**

● Foreign investors are very much like American firms investing abroad: they
  are large, vertically and horizontally integrated firms seeking to exploit what
  economists call "ownership advantages"—that is, management and marketing skills, technology, and other know-how. Foreign firms come here for many
  reasons: to capture and hold markets, to avoid protectionism, to tap technology and our skilled labor force, to take advantage of our open door policy
  towards foreign direct investment (FDI) and our political stability.[2] When
  the dollar dropped, after 1985, there was an added advantage: American assets
  were at fire sale prices.

● It is not the size but the rate of growth of FDI that stands out (Figure 4.2).
  Foreign investment grew by 17 percent per year during the 1980s. As we mention shortly, FDI remains but a small part of the vast American economy.

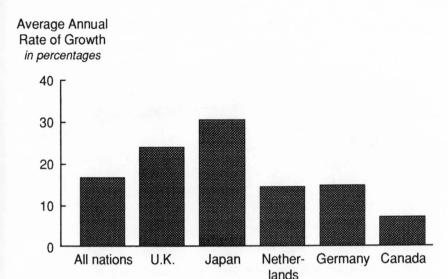

Average Annual
Rate of Growth
in percentages

Source: U.S. Department of Commerce, Office of Trade and International Investment

Figure 4.2   Growth of FDIUS by Country, 1980–86

● FDI is fundamentally a takeover phenomenon, with little new plant construction. Between 1981 and 1987 more than four of five dollars directly invested in this country were in the form of mergers and acquisitions. In 1986, 97 percent of the employment added to foreign payrolls was through acquisitions (Figure 4.3). Some foreign takeovers have been friendly (like News Corporation's takeover of Triangle Publications), some unfriendly (Grant Metropolitan's acquisition of Pillsbury). On occasion, foreigners have been "white knights," saving an American company from a hostile takeover (e.g., Yamanouchi's buy out of Shaklee to rescue it from Irwin Jacobs). The Japanese have been different from other investors in that they have been most likely to build new plants and thus increase employment. But this situation is beginning to change. Japanese investors are increasingly getting into the merger and acquisition movement, like their British, Canadian, and Dutch counterparts. Bridgestone's 1988 purchase of Firestone is an example of the Japanese acquisition wave.

● Most foreign investment is in manufacturing—especially chemicals, rubber, printing and publishing, autos, and cement (Figure 4.4). There is also much

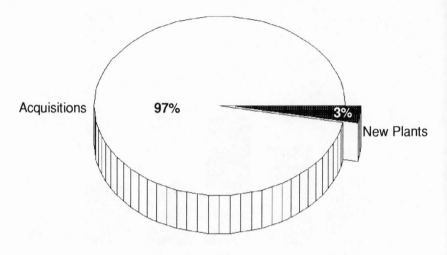

Source: *Survey of Current Business,* May 1986

Figure 4.3   Foreign Investment Is Predominantly a Takeover Phenomenon—Percentage of Employment Added, 1986

foreign investment in natural resources. Recently, there have been substantial increases in the services—particularly advertising and finance. Finally, there has been a considerable increase in real estate investment, especially in residential property in Hawaii and in office buildings in Los Angeles, Washington, New York, Atlanta, and Houston. (This investment is the most visible kind and the one that upsets many Americans so much.)

●   Foreign investment has had a stronger impact in some regions than in the nation as a whole. Historically, FDIUS has been concentrated in the East coast and the South. Over time, however, investment has fanned out across the country. Between 1974 and 1986, the fastest-growing regions for foreign investment were the Southeast, Southwest, Rocky Mountains, Plains, and Far West. Importantly, when we look only at acquisitions, we find them overwhelmingly in the North. New plants and expansions of existing plants—the kinds of foreign investments that create jobs—were concentrated in the South.

●   Some foreigners are good employers and have solid labor relations with their employees, such as Toyota in its joint venture with General Motors in Fremont, California. On the other hand, some foreigners have engaged in ad-

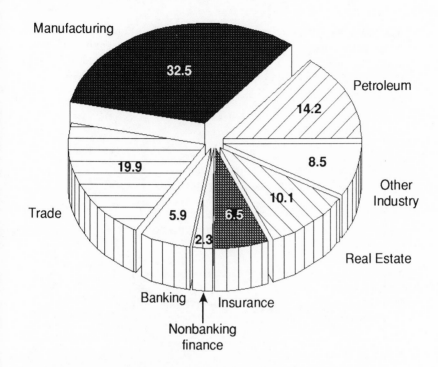

Source: *Survey of Current Business,* June 1987

Figure 4.4   Distribution of FDIUS by Industry, 1986

versarial and illegal labor relations practices. (Again, so do American employers.) It is hard to define a "foreign model" of labor relations. Overall, foreign and American firms seem to have similar industrial relations.

A mixed picture of foreign investors emerges from close inspection of them. In many ways they act like their American counterparts in size, organization, and operating style. Yet, there are differences as well, particularly in the management style of Japanese companies.

ARE WE LOSING CONTROL OF THE AMERICAN ECONOMY?

With these facts as background, let us return to the question raised by the economic nationalists: Are we selling off our national assets and surrendering our sovereignty to foreigners? The answer is a qualified no. U.S. Department of

Commerce data show that foreign ownership of American companies is still relatively small. Only about 3.5 percent of our workers and 8 percent of our productive assets are under foreign control (Figure 4.5). In manufacturing, foreign penetration is higher—8 percent of employment and 12 percent of assets.

Percentage

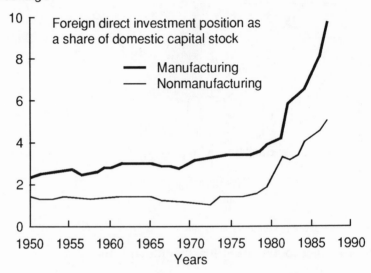

Figure 4.5   **Foreign Ownership of American Capital, 1950–87**

These are relatively small numbers compared with other countries (such as West Germany and Canada), but much larger than others like Japan. They are also much larger than at the beginning of the decade. And, there is a strong likelihood that foreign companies will buy considerably more assets in the near future if the low value of the dollar persists. The decline in the dollar since 1985 was a product the United States' giant trade and budget deficits and mismanaged economic policy. If there is considerably more direct investment, we may have to worry—especially if it is in economically and militarily strategic industries.

One area of concern to many is banking and finance, the nerve center of the economy. Over 20 percent of our banking assets are already in foreign-controlled banks, up sharply from only a few years ago.[3] Since banking is strategically important, many feel uneasy about this level of penetration. Concern has also been voiced over foreign purchases of defense contractors, especially in ceramics, on the grounds of national security, although several buy outs in recent years have had Pentagon approval. Foreign investment is also strong in chemicals, cement, and publishing. In the first two cases, a few foreign companies now control more than 40 percent of American assets and some observers are concerned on anti-trust grounds. In publishing, the large takeovers of major houses (like Doubleday) by foreigners have obvious and potentially serious implications for that industry and for the molding of American public opinion. In addition, there is concern with the growing political clout foreigners can now wield (of course, we also should be concerned with undue political influence of American companies).

Does this influx of investment from abroad pose a danger to our economic security? We have no magic number about how much is *too* much foreign investment. Nor does anyone else. It is very difficult to define national security—as the federal Committee on Foreign Investment in the United States has found. CFIUS is the intragency group responsible for reviewing foreign investment in strategically important industries. However, it does appear that a "takeover" is very far in the future. In many ways, focusing on the issue of foreign "control" misses more important issues.

FOREIGN JOB CREATION: LESS THAN MEETS THE EYE

Since, in general, foreign companies have only a small degree of control over American assets, it is not surprising that their contribution to American employment is also small. But one fallacy pervades the popular press more than any other: that foreigners have created millions of jobs in the United States. It is true that almost three million Americans worked for foreign-owned companies in 1987, compared with only one million in 1974. But that does not mean that foreigners generated two million new jobs.

The enormous confusion over this issue is in large part because of a fundamental misreading of the data. Our research shows clearly that *all* of the employment added to foreign payrolls is through acquisitions and mergers. Mergers and acquisitions (M&A) primarily represent the shift of employment from American to foreign owners. Here, foreigners do not *create* new jobs—they simply *control* more. At worst, a foreign acquisition can result in the diversion of resources to speculative and unproductive uses and corporate restructuring and job loss because of the debt incurred by the acquisition; at best it can lead to an expansion and more jobs. In this regard, foreign M&A activity is no different from that of American companies.

Little investment comes through the establishment of new plants. Without doubt, these start-ups add to the number of jobs in the economy. The Japanese have led all countries in green field investments. They are the only major investing nation with more new plant announcements than mergers and acquisitions. The most often-cited example of job creation through new plants comes from the Japanese auto industry. Honda's Marysville, Ohio, factory, started in 1982, was the first

Japanese auto transplant.[4] By the late 1980s, Honda employed over five thousand workers and planned to add thousands more by the early 1990s in two more Ohio plants. Nissan employed 3,200 workers in Smyrna, Tennessee, by 1988 and every major Japanese automaker played "follow the leader" by setting up its own assembly plants. Toyota, Mitsubishi, and Isuzu also built new facilities. These Japanese plants evoked an image of foreign start-ups sprouting jobs like wildflowers in spring.

But the reality is far different. A careful reading of U.S. Department of Commerce data dampens the excitement and fascination for foreign transplants. These numbers show that new foreign-owned establishments created only 90 thousand jobs from 1980 through 1987, or an average of 11 thousand jobs a year. The annual numbers vary widely, however, as Figure 4.6 shows. New establishment generated 14,072 jobs in 1981, but only 4,139 in 1984. The lower job gains in the mid-1980s were partly because of the strong dollar and the deep recession of 1982-83. By 1987, new establishment jobs were rising: foreigners created 15,083 jobs that year.[5] These small numbers—compared to the size of the U.S. economy—contradict the notion that foreign start-ups are reindustrializing the country. Even if one assumes a very large multiplier effect, new foreign plants cannot be responsible for more than 30 to 40 thousand jobs a year, a tiny sum in an economy with more than 100 million workers.

Purchases from suppliers generate considerable additional jobs. Yet, these local linkages may be smaller for foreign than for domestic firms because foreigners often buy their inputs from their plants at home. Imports to the United States are high among foreign companies. One study estimated that the average Japanese automobile assembly plant in this country generated fewer than three supplier jobs for every assembly job, compared with a more than a four-to-one ratio for the average domestic automobile plant in the United States (Howes, 1986).

But there is some evidence that local supply linkages for foreigners are growing as foreigners build more supplier plants. By 1988, more than 200 Japanese auto parts makers had followed on the heels of the Japanese MNCs. Experts project that 300 parts makers will have set up operations by 1990 (Arnesen, Coles, and Krishna, 1987). Some American-owned companies in the Mid-South and Mid-West also benefited from the presence of Mazda and Toyota, especially since General Motors, Ford, and Chrysler are buying more of their parts offshore. On the other hand, many of the new competitors displaced American suppliers as they retained their ties to their traditional Japanese partners and successfully captured some of the business of our own Big Three. In an era of overcapacity in this industry, there is likely to be a shakeout in the auto supply industry. Many of the displaced will be domestic suppliers, going down in defeat on their own playing field, overcome by foreign companies. So, the effect of new foreign-owned plants on supply operations is ambiguous: they buy local inputs and create additional jobs, but they also compete with and sometimes displace workers in domestic firms.

The source of most of job creation is not from new plants, but through expansions of existing facilities. In 1987, for example, Honda embarked on a $450 million

Number of
Employees
in thousands

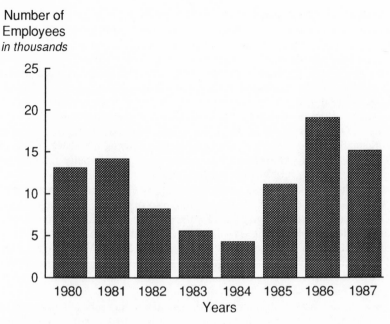

Source: Bureau of Economic Analysis

**Figure 4.6   Employment from New Foreign Establishments,
1980–87**

expansion to boost its American engine production capacity sixfold and to start
producing transmissions, suspension assemblies, and brakes. According to the
Bureau of Economic Analysis, for affiliates with more than 500 employees,
expansions of existing plants added nearly 300 thousand additional employees.[6]
When we factor in smaller affiliates, the most optimistic figure for total jobs added
to American payrolls through new plants and expansions is 351,308.[7] This sounds
like a lot of jobs. It *appears* plausible that hundreds of thousands, perhaps even
millions, of jobs were generated since the boom began in the 1970s. Through new
plants and plant expansions, foreigners *directly* created about 75 thousand jobs a
year. A generous multiplier would perhaps triple that figure.

But there is more to tell. Like American companies, foreigners close plants and
lay off workers. Since foreign investment is always a risky and uncertain venture, this should not be a complete surprise. Many foreign enterprises are forced
to scale back or drop out of U.S. competition. Despite expectations of high market penetration in America, optimistic plans often do not pan out. Even Japanese
companies, like Sumitomo Chemical Company and Tokyo Print Industries, have
retreated or withdrawn. Some Japanese manufacturing companies have suffered

continued losses, failing to meet with the kind of success they anticipated in America. Some estimate that as many as four of five Japanese factories are unprofitable (Gumbel and Sease, 1987:6; *Japan Economic Journal* Staff, 1986:13). But clearly many "patient" foreign multinationals are in the United States for the long haul and are willing to hang in here until they make profits. But just as there are expansions, there are also plant closures and layoffs.

No case better illustrates this than Volkswagen. When Volkswagen opened its Pennsylvania factory in 1978, it held some of the "ownership" advantages economists say are necessary to motivate direct investment. Volkswagen was a specialist in small car production, increasingly popular during the energy crisis of the 1970s. The company enjoyed strong consumer loyalty, especially among baby boomers who made the company's inexpensive, yet reliable Beetle a cult phenomenon in the 1960s. And Volkswagen, partially state-owned, was a model of German efficiency. Yet these advantages failed to make VW's Rabbits, Golfs, and Jettas winners in the United States By the mid-1980s sales were continually eroding and the troubled Pennsylvania plant operated at less than one-third of capacity. Finally, after a 10-year struggle in the United States, Volkswagen abandoned the factory in 1988, leaving 25 hundred employees jobless. The multiplier increased job loss in the region even more. The immense subsidies that Pennsylvania paid to entice VW were largely dissipated.

So far we have left aside the employment potential of mergers and acquisitions because it is difficult to measure accurately. Without better data than are currently available, it is often hard to tell precisely what happens when Grand Metropolitan buys Pillsbury or Seagrams buys Tropicana. In some instances, foreign takeovers rescue the acquired corporations and save American jobs. In other cases acquisitions restructure and liquidate U.S. companies, thus eliminating employment.

Consider first the positive side. If we ignore divestitures and liquidations for a minute, foreigners added 2.2 million jobs to their payrolls from 1980 to 1987 through U.S. acquisitions and mergers. This is over 25 times the amount of employment they created through new plants.[8] As we have said, acquisitions may preserve jobs in failing American firms poised to shut down unless revived with infusions of capital.

U.S. jobs can also be lost through acquisitions and subsequent divestitures. The Canadian raider Robert Campeau provides an interesting example of the acquisitor-divestor in action. In 1986, his real estate firm, the Campeau Corporation, with $188 million in sales, bought the giant retail clothing chain, Allied Stores. Here, a little fish swallowed a huge fish. Allied had sales of $4.5 billion that year. Through this transaction, Robert Campeau got two things. First, he took control of some of this country's premier clothing stores, including the high-toned Brooks Brothers, Bonwit Teller, and Ann Taylor. Second, Campeau took on an enormous amount of debt, a direct result of this little fish's big meal. Campeau owed a staggering $1.1 billion by the end of 1988, with much more due later. To meet these debts, Campeau quickly sold off 16 of 24 divisions within a few months:

Bonwit Teller went to Australia's Hooker, Garfinkel's to Raleigh's, and Joske's to Dillard's. These fire sales raised about $750 million for Campeau by August 1987. He kept only a few jewels like Brooks Brothers and Ann Taylor.

But the important news for our story is that four thousand Allied Stores workers lost their jobs when the company was "restructured to pay off the debt" (Benjamin, 1988). The Allied story also shows how easy it is to misread the data on foreign investment. In tabulating the Allied deal, the Commerce Department reported that the number of Americans working for foreign companies went up by the number of those employed by Campeau's Allied after the divestiture. To the casual observer, this seems to add a significant number of people to foreign payrolls. But, as things turned out, there was net job loss as a result of the divestiture. More people had jobs controlled by foreign companies, but fewer Allied people had jobs.

However, the Campeau story did not end with his capture and dispersal of Allied's assets. Early in 1988, he launched the biggest retailing takeover bid in history by offering $6.6 billion in a bitter battle for Federated Department Stores, the country's second largest retailer. To pull off this acquisition, Campeau sold off Brooks Brothers (to England's Marks and Spencer) and Ann Taylor, the two remaining jewels of the Allied acquisition, and, even before completing the deal, arranged to divest $4.4 billion of Federated's assets (see Cook and Terry, 1987; Hagedorn, 1987; Power and Terry, 1986; and Rose and Hagedorn, 1987). During the spring of 1988, Campeau was looking at laying off enough workers to save $160 million. Within a month or two of the takeover of Federated, Campeau fired 3,547 workers: he slashed Bloomingdale's staff by nearly one-third, cut 794 jobs at Abraham and Strauss, 250 at Rich's in Atlanta, 1,200 at Lazarus, 320 at Burdine's, and 600 (25 percent of all workers) at Goldsmith's, among others (Hansard, 1988). This was only the beginning of what industry experts believe will be wholesale layoffs (Hymowitz, 1988). By the end of 1988, Campeau had laid off more than eight thousand workers from Allied and Federated (Hansard, 1988). Early in 1990, Campeau filed for bankruptcy. So, even though Commerce Department data showed an increased number of workers employed by foreign companies because of the two takeovers, there was a decrease in employment as a result of Campeau's acquisitions and divestitures.

THE UNEVEN RECORD OF JOB EXPANSION AND CUTBACKS

Thus foreign acquisitors are buying into and selling out of America. How many jobs are actually created by foreign companies, once we account for mergers and acquisitions, divestitures and cutbacks? According to the Bureau of Economic Analysis, foreigners added 547,931 jobs to their payrolls between 1982 and 1986.[9] This employment results from more than just the balance between new plants and expansions, on one hand, and cutbacks on the other. It also comes through acquisitions and divestitures (sales and liquidations) of companies. Since acquisitions are much larger than new plants and expansions, we have to take account of their effect on employment. However, these jobs were not new jobs, but mostly represent only takeovers of American companies—the transfer of control from American to foreign owners.

Let's look at Figure 4.7 to understand how many of these jobs were new and how many were only the result of selling American assets to foreign companies, a transfer of control. Think of the process as a job employment "pool" into which jobs "pour in" through two faucets at the top and "flow out" through two drains at the bottom.[10] An interesting and clear picture emerges.

First, let's look at the faucet at the upper left of Figure 4.7. We see new plants (45,151) and plant expansions (341,281) poured in over 386 thousand new jobs. These are unambiguously new jobs created in the U.S. economy. But, in addition, acquisitions from the right hand faucet added almost 1.4 million more. Some of them represented jobs saved by foreigners who bought American plants that would have been shut down by their owners because of poor performance. Other jobs simply represent the transfer of ownership from American to foreign companies. It is impossible to tell exactly how many of these jobs were saved and how many were transfers from one owner to another, but the latter is probably more prevalent. At any rate, taken together, new plants, plant expansions and acquisitions increased the potential foreign job pool by 1,768,122 workers between 1982 and 1986.

Now let's look at what happens at the bottom of the pool, as cutbacks and sales and liquidations of firms "drain" jobs. Cutbacks from existing plants drained off more than 442 thousand jobs. As the multiplier worked to increase jobs through added purchases when foreigners created direct jobs, so the multiplier works to reduce (indirect) supplier jobs when cutbacks occur. Unfortunately, the BEA's reporting scheme lumps together sales and liquidations, so we cannot separate the two categories. Unquestionably, liquidations of firms mean jobs lost. But the largest part of this category is sales.[11] When a foreign firm sells some assets, it is impossible to say much about job change. The new owner might save them and rebuild the company or might eventually close it down. Like the circumstances involving the "saving" of jobs through foreign acquisitions, it is impossible to tell whether or not there is job loss. All the data allow us to say is that sales and liquidations of firms taken together resulted in almost 778 thousand fewer jobs. So, when we finish pouring in new plants, expansions, and acquisitions from the faucets and siphon off jobs from cutbacks and sales and liquidations through the drain, we have a total increase in the pool of 547,927. The left hand side of Figure 4.7 shows that if foreign investment were only a matter of new plants and expansions and cutbacks, there would have been a *net loss* of jobs from the economy of close to 56 thousand jobs (jobs gained in new plants and expansions minus those lost in cutbacks).

Therefore, FDIUS spawns jobs and destroys them too. The net result for 1982–86, though, is job loss unless one assumes that acquisitions saved jobs that would have been lost if the acquired U.S. firm went out of business. There is simply no

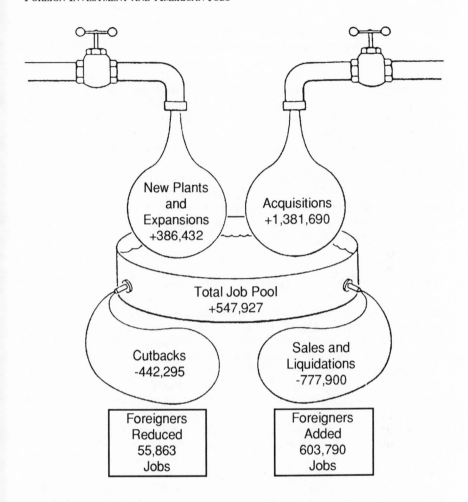

Source: U.S. Department of Commerce, Bureau of Economic Analysis

Figure 4.7   Do Foreigners Create New Jobs?

evidence that this is true. Therefore, the net gain in foreign employment in the economy is strictly through takeover activity. Acquisitions are responsible for whatever gains are attributable to foreigners. Given this, we can hardly call foreigners ''saviors'' of American industry. But we can understand why the press and the public think that foreigners are adding jobs to the economy. The press, alas, is wrong.

The time period we examined (the only years for which data are available) included 1982–83, part of the deepest recession since the 1930s. Foreigners fired 140 thousand workers that year. Of course, American firms also laid off workers—about 1.6 million during the lean years of the early 1980s. To get a sense of what happened after the recession ended, we calculated the net jobs change for 1984 to 1986, when 5.1 million jobs added nationwide. What did foreigners contribute to this jobs boom? There was a net increase of only 55,510 jobs (the employment gains from new plants and plant expansions minus cutbacks), an average of just under 18.5 thousand per year.[12] Foreigners contributed less than 1 percent of all U.S. job growth from 1984 to 1986. This was a period of strong employment growth and considerable attention was paid to the reindustrialization potential of FDIUS. So even in upswings, the U.S. economy is not getting many more new jobs in the bargain. In terms of the large American job pool, foreigners added only a few drops. But, at least, they were adding jobs when the economy was more robust.

FOREIGN INVESTMENT AND THE TRADE DEFICIT

Along with job creation, another common misconception about foreign investment concerns its effect on the balance of trade. Anecdotes about foreign companies exporting their U.S.-made products began turning up in the press in 1988. Honda, for example, launched a big publicity campaign about its first shipments of cars to Japan in 1988 (Bussey, 1987). Japanese and other foreign companies trumpet their contributions to the reduction of the U.S. trade deficit through these exports. Siemens showed TV ads claiming that 15 percent of its U.S. production was exported. Although there are limited examples of these exports, a look at aggregate data on foreigners' exports and imports show a very different picture. The "New Competitors" have increased, not decreased, our trade deficit.

We mentioned earlier that many believe that foreigners import much of their inputs. In 1986, the United States had a merchandise trade deficit of $149 billion, according to the Bureau of Economic Analysis. That year, foreign affiliates imported $124 billion and exported only $51 billion, for a net deficit of $73 billion. Much of this took place through wholesalers who imported goods from their overseas suppliers for sale in the United States. Foreign wholesalers accounted for nearly $58 billion of that deficit. This situation reflects the ability of foreign companies to import successfully—it is more of a trade than an investment phenomenon. After all, American wholesalers are also importing goods from foreign sources. But, leaving aside wholesale operations, foreign firms imported $15.8 billion more than they exported. This amounts to nearly 11 percent of the entire merchandise trade balance, although we believe this to be an underestimate of foreigners' contribution to the trade deficit.[13] Most of the nonwholesaling deficit, $8.8 billion, was represented by the trade deficit of manufacturers alone. For every dollar of exports by foreign affiliates manufacturers, there were $1.65 in imports during 1986. Thus, anecdotal evidence about foreign investment turns out to be untrue.

FOREIGN INVESTORS' CONTRIBUTION TO THE ECONOMY

Despite foreigners' limited contribution of job creation and their negative contribution to the trade deficit, they have contributed to the economy in a number of key respects. For starters, foreign firms paid out $87 billion in employee compensation in 1986. One Commerce Department analyst estimates that foreigners paid about 25 percent more per worker than U.S.-owned companies, although precise comparisons between American and foreign companies are difficult to make because of data restrictions.[14] Foreigners' higher wages are partly because they are concentrated in oligopolistic manufacturing industries which pay higher-than-average wages. FDI also raises hopes for new jobs, new technology, and new management expertise. After Hitachi announced a plant opening in Norman in 1985, the move "made headlines almost equal to the first man on the moon," says former Oklahoma governor George Nigh who actively recruited the firm (Mason and Hoerr, 1988). Some foreign firms have even become exporters although, as we will show, they have been on the whole net importers.

Foreign companies have also been active in many industries abandoned by American firms. Even steel, the symbol of America's atrophied smokestack industry, saw a foreign-led industrial renaissance. In 1984, for example, Japan's Kawasaki Steel and Brazil's Companhia Vale do Rio Doce bought a plant from Kaiser Steel and renamed it California Steel. A California economic development official said, "You wouldn't have a steel industry in this state if it were not for foreign investment" (Koepp, 1987:59).[15] Nippon Kokan Steel has been pumping new technology into its partner National Steel. The resurgence of the American foundry was capped when Inland Steel and Japan's Nippon Steel announced I/N Tek in 1987. This joint venture created a state-of-the-art steel mill in New Carlisle, Indiana, prompting Indiana Lieutenant Governor John Mutz to declare that, "The very future of domestic steel depends on investment like this" (Belsie, 1987:7). Mutz's message resonates throughout the country.

European companies have also had a positive effect on industrial restructuring. Early in the 1980s, Britain's leading electronics firm, Plessey, set its sights on the thriving American telecommunications equipment market. It acquired Stromberg-Carlson. Yet the 1982 takeover "drew more laughs than a Monty Python movie," for Stromberg-Carlson was a "stodgy little money-loser, suffering from a succession of owners, an unfocused strategy, and a boring product line" (Keller, 1987:32). However, through superior management and technology the British investors revitalized this once-listless firm. Now it appears that Plessey is getting the last laugh. By the mid-1980s, with the managerial and technical help it needed from its overseas parent, Stromberg-Carlson was turning a healthy profit and now commands a significant share of the U.S. telecommunications switch-

ing equipment business. Bridgestone's takeover of Firestone is another example
of an acquisition in which capital and expertise revived an American firm.

It is clear, then, that foreign multinationals may revitalize American industry
by introducing new technology, managerial skills, and labor practices. Perhaps
the best example is the just-in-time inventory system (JIT). Japanese firms have
introduced the JIT system to minimize inventories and cut costs. Many U.S. firms
later adopted JIT. Foreign firms have also demonstrated that it is still possible to
produce efficiently in the United States, even in smokestack industries once thought
to be in irreversible decline. The objective of I/N Tek, for instance, is to slash
the production time of cold-rolled steel by 90 percent.

Not only have there been investments by foreign MNCs, there has also been
substantial involvement by these companies in our political and cultural life that
goes far beyond job creation (Malcolm, 1988). More sushi and schnitzel appear
on restaurant menus, language classes abound, and local arts programs contain
more opera and less bluegrass. Corporate leaders have also become heavily involved in philanthropy. One report in 1988 placed Japanese philanthropy at $140
million (Holstein, 1988). A Nissan executive ran Nashville's United Way drive
in 1985. In Charlotte, North Carolina, foreigners, who comprise 7 percent of the
population, are major supporters of an opera and symphony orchestra (which has
a Dutch conductor). Canadian business firms endow academic chairs in Canadian studies, as other countries do for the study of their cultures. Japan's Mitsui
and Mitsubishi have endowed 16 chairs at U.S. universities. MIT alone has created over a dozen academic chairs funded by Japanese multinationals (Helm, 1988).

IS FOREIGN INVESTMENT A PROBLEM?

We have seen that foreign investment is neither a major threat to our economic
sovereignty nor an engine of job creation. Overall, the greater internationalization of the economy—of which foreign investment is an important part—is not
strictly "good" or "bad" for the United States. However, internationalization
makes economic decision making more complicated and difficult. As a result,
FDI is in no means a "nonproblem," but requires attention from governments,
corporations, and organized labor.

We believe that foreign investment requires policies for a number of important reasons. First, increasing foreign domination *could* result if current trends
are allowed to continue. Greater foreign investment certainly will take place if
the dollar falls back to early-1989 levels or lower values. The devalued dollar, in
turn, is a product of our massive trade and federal budget deficits; these "twin
deficits" are products of misguided economic policy. We are particularly concerned about the growing domination of foreign companies in some concentrated
industries like chemicals or cement. Second, foreign investment has grown rapidly because of failures of government and corporate policies and reflects our loss

of competitiveness. The federal government has failed to respond decisively to the growing mobility of international capital and its economic consequences. As we face the 1990s, U.S. policies remain inert, ineffective, or inconsistent. They are predicated on out-dated notions of laissez faire and "free trade" which are of little relevance in today's world (see Prestowitz, 1988). The time to start shaping a long-run strategy toward foreign investment—more importantly, toward a revitalization of the economy—should come before the fears about foreign domination become reality. Present policies should be replaced by those that give us a more productive economy and encourage more productive (rather than acquisitional) foreign investment in the United States.

Second, important private-sector problems have allowed great penetration of the economy. America has important internal problems—the result of short-term business planning horizons, lack of long-run investment commitments, and slow economic and productivity growth. Trade unions too have not been as adaptable to foreign competition—at home or abroad—as they should. In general, our economy has not been flexible enough and has reacted too slowly to major changes in the international arena.

Third, is the sorry fact that much of the burden of dealing with foreign investment has been relegated to state and local governments which are not able to handle it. By treating FDI in effect as a nonproblem, the federal government has pitted the states and localities—who are often desperate to attract new jobs—against powerful multinational corporations. The MNCs are easily able to play one off against the other and extract gigantic subsidies to locate in particular places. For example, Toyota got about $100 thousand per job from Kentucky for putting its plant in Georgetown, Kentucky. Having three thousand governments making much of our international investment policy is ludicrous. A more active role on the part of the federal government is necessary.

Our policy proposals fall into six major categories:[16]

1. **Closing the ignorance gap**. The building blocks of any policy lie in the information needed to formulate it. At present, the federal government lacks critical data needed to understand FDI. The United States must gather all pertinent information about direct investment needed to measure its effects and to formulate effective policy. Without more information on the activities of foreign companies—especially their job-creating activities—we cannot formulate decent policy at the national or the state and local levels. We can collect more information without publicly disclosing information on individual companies. Further, we should create a permanent federal review board that analyzes the economic impacts of major investments and reports to other federal agencies and to state development organizations that are attempting to attract FDI.

2. **Restoring international competitiveness**. At present, foreign firms are primarily attracted to America's market, not its productive climate. The federal government must play a stronger role in creating a basis for long-term, capacity-building investment and better job opportunities. It can do this by primarily investing

in human resources—education and training, research and development, and so on—and physical infrastructure—highways, telecommunications, et cetera—to encourage the flow of foreign investment into productive uses over the long run. Such policies will also help keep American investment at home by making it more profitable for our multinationals to produce domestically.

Also, our firms and our governments must revise their views not only of these "invading" foreigners, but of the way that we manage our firms and our economy. We must refocus our economic and management policies and increase investment and productivity in a more competitive economic environment. Importantly, the propensity for American companies to think about the next quarter's profits rather than the next decade's new products and market share must change. The tendency towards mergers and acquisitions rather than concentration on new products and processes must be reversed, too. The country must take a *strategic, long-term* approach to economic policy—in board rooms, government offices, and union halls.

3. **Controlling the dual deficits**. More than anything else, the federal budget and international trade deficits have made U.S. economy increasingly dependent on foreign capital. We need policies to reduce the federal deficit and still pay for new programs to restore competitiveness. This will require new taxes and cuts in some existing programs. In addition, the United States must move beyond exchange rate manipulation to reduce the foreign trade deficit. We must put more energy and resources into promoting U.S. exports, solve the Third World debt problem, and get more cooperation from our allies on the coordination of economic and defense policies.

4. **Beefing up merger and antitrust policy**. Foreigners have piled up financial assets through the massive trade deficits we have run during the 1980s. These assets now help fuel an unprecedented merger and acquisition binge. In turn, foreign companies are gaining significant control over some U.S. markets. As a necessary complement to policies designed to restore real productive investment in plants and equipment, the federal government must enforce policies to discourage uncompetitive practices and unproductive merger and acquisition activity.

5. **Reducing the competition among states and localities for foreign investment**. States and localities are at a distinct disadvantage in bidding among each other for relatively few foreign jobs. These governments need to form alliances to reduce wasteful incentives and to structure them more effectively; to use performance requirements and "clawback" provisions to get more local jobs out of their incentives; and more efficiently to make local economic development policies.

6. **Developing "exit" policy and plant-closing legislation**. Any program for economic growth must also involve a program for economic security. The tendency of foreign and domestic firms to shift capital rapidly around the globe exacerbates job insecurity. Thus, America's open door for multinational entry must

be balanced by a multinational "exit" policy when firms relocate abroad and displace workers here. Apart from federal and state job retraining programs, the best policy is a uniform national standard for plant closings and layoffs for large firms—including longer advance notification of plant closings, job severance pay, and adjustment assistance to workers and communities afflicted by job loss.

These policies, taken together, will provide more opportunity for profits and jobs. They are aimed not only at foreign investors but at our own investors as well. If we build a stronger economy based on productive investment rather than debt-driven demand we will not have to worry about foreigners. If the economy is healthy, foreigners are more likely to make investments that create jobs—as they did from 1984 to 1986.

In the end, foreign investment is a phenomenon that offers a mixture of new opportunities and challenges—for jobs and social and political change. Much of our economic future in this country depends critically on how we handle inward (and outward) foreign investment. These policies will affect our jobs, our incomes, and our political relations. Americans simply cannot understand the way our economy works without getting a better picture of foreign investment.

In the final analysis, foreigners are here to stay—they are a growing part of our economy, and will remain so for a long time to come. In many ways they are no different from our own corporations. With foreign-based multinationals increasing their position in America and U.S. multinationals shipping products into the United States from offshore, it is no longer possible to say what is "foreign" and what is "American." The distinction between where a product is developed, produced, and assembled is blurred since "The Global Factory" can disperse these functions throughout the world. For the same reasons, the relationship between the corporation and nation has been significantly broken (see Reich, 1988). What is the relationship between BASF AG, the German parent of the U.S. affiliate and the Germany economy? Is Nestle, which derives but 2 percent of its sales from Switzerland, really a "Swiss" corporation except in the location of its headquarters and the laws under which its by-laws are written? Similarly, as IBM and Ford buy more of their components overseas, what is their connection—and their commitment—to the American economy? By definition, multinationals span national boundaries and transcend nations and national interests. We have, therefore, to rethink the fundamental idea that a country and its corporations have consistent interests. Or that foreign-based MNCs are not necessarily "less American" than "American" MNCs.

Notes

This chapter draws from the authors' book *The New Competitors: How Foreign Investors Are Changing the U.S. Economy* (New York: Basic Books, 1989).

1. Foreign direct investment is defined as a "U.S. business affiliate in which a single foreign person owns or controls, directly or indirectly, 10 percent or more of the voting

securities of an incorporated business enterprise or an equivalent interest in an unincorporated enterprise.'' See Howenstine (1987, p. 36).

2. On analyses of international direct investment, see Hymer (1976). For appraisals of his lasting contribution to the theory of FDI, see Caves (1982), Dunning and Rugman (1985), Kindleberger (1969), and Teece (1985). For other discussions of FDI, see Chaudhuri (1983), Drucker (1987:26), Dunning (1981), Hirsch (1967), Hymer (1972), Schoenberger (1986), and Vernon (1966, 1971:4, 1974).

3. The 20 percent figure includes foreign bank holdings of foreign assets, so it overstates foreign control of American assets.

4. Actually, the plant produced motorcycles beginning in the late 1970s. Auto production began in 1982.

5. For annual data on employment from new foreign establishment, see the May issues of *Survey of Current Business*. See, for example, Herr (1988). We obtained revised data for 1980–84 from the Bureau of Economic Analysis (BEA). Note that these new establishment jobs may include plant expansions. Also, they are somewhat inflated because foreigners often report an anticipated job count that never actually reaches the tally provided to the BEA.

6. The government provides employment from expanded operations for large plants for only 1982 to 1986.

7. We explain this and the calculations that follow in detail in Appendix B of *The New Competitors*.

8. We tallied these data from Herr (1988) and supplementary information supplied by the Bureau of Economic Analysis. The figures reported, however, are inflated because many firms divested assets after the BEA compiled employment information.

9. We only analyzed 1982–86 data because these are the only years that the BEA breaks out the components of employment change: employment from new plants, expansions, cutbacks, and sales and liquidations. For more detail, see Appendix B to *The New Competitors*.

10. The BEA data give consistent breakdowns of new plants and plant expansions, acquisitions, sales and liquidations, and cutbacks only for affiliates with 500 or more employees. Activities of smaller affiliates are not covered consistently. However, since the larger companies account for some 90 percent of all affiliate employment, results presented here are not likely to be far off. We made estimates of the breakdowns for the smaller affiliates, as we show in Appendix B of *The New Competitors*.

11. Telephone interview with Ned Howenstine of the Bureau of Economic Analysis, June, 1988.

12. Once again, we leave out the net effects of acquisitions and mergers and sales and liquidations for the reasons discussed earlier.

13. This figuring leaves out the Japanese wholesalers who own manufacturing plants and bring in auto parts for their manufacturing operations. Honda's manufacturing operations are a subsidiary of its wholesaling company and its manufacturing employees are counted as wholesaling workers. So, our figures underestimate the extent of their imports.

14. See Coleman (1986). Our comparison of average hourly wages from the Bureau of Economic Analysis *1980 Benchmark Survey of Foreign Investment in the United States*

(U.S. Bureau of the Census, 1983) and roughly comparable figures from the *1980–81 Annual Survey of Manufactures* (U.S. Bureau of the Census, 1984) shows much less difference between foreign and domestic companies. As we show elsewhere, the published data are too primitive to make decent approximations between foreign and domestic firms.

15. Although saved from closing, the company changed dramatically, from an integrated mill to one that made only rolled steel. Employment was cut too.

16. These policies are spelled out in greater detail in *The New Competitors*, Chapters 9 and 10.

References

Arnesen, Peter, Robert Coles, and A. Rama Krishna (1987) "Japanese Auto Parts Companies in the U.S. and Japan: Implications for U.S. Competitors." Ann Arbor: East Asian Business Program, University of Michigan.

Belsie, Laurent (1987) "Japanese Steel Companies in U.S. to Stay." *Christian Science Monitor* (25 March):7.

Benjamin, Daniel (1988) "New Miracle on 34th Street?" *Time* 131 (14 March):51.

Business Week Staff (1984) "How Overseas Investors Are Helping to Reindustrialize America." *Business Week* (4 June):103–04.

Bussey, John (1987) "Honda Outlines Big Expansion of Its U.S. Unit." *Wall Street Journal* (18 September):52.

Caves, Richard (1982) *Multinational Enterprise and Economic Analysis*. Cambridge, England: Cambridge University Press.

Chaudhuri, Adhip (1983) "American Multinationals and American Employment." In *The Multinational Corporation in the 1980s*, edited by Charles P. Kindleberger and David B. Audretsch, 263–77. Cambridge, MA: MIT Press.

Coleman, Edwin J. (1986) "Regional Aspects of Foreign Direct Investment." Paper presented at the Southern Regional Science Association meetings. Washington, DC: Bureau of Economic Analysis, U.S. Department of Commerce.

Collier, June M. (1988) "Foreign Money Is Bad for USA." *USA Today* (17 August):10A.

Cook, Dan with Edith Terry and Amy Dunkin (1987) "Is Campeau in over His Head at Allied Stores?" *Business Week* (9 February):52–53

Drucker, Peter F. (1987) "From World Trade to World Investment." *Wall Street Journal* (26 May):32.

Dunning, John H. (1981) *International Production and the Multinational Enterprise*. New York: Praeger.

Dunning, John H. and Alan M. Rugman (1985) "The Influence of Hymer's Dissertation on the Theory of Foreign Direct Investment." *American Economic Review* 75(2):228–32.

Forbes, Malcolm S. (1988) "Before Japan Buys Too Much of the U.S.A." *Forbes* 141 (25 January):17.

Glickman, Norman J. and Douglas P. Woodward (1989) *The New Competitors: How Foreign Investors Are Changing the U.S. Economy.* New York: Basic Books.

Gumbel, Peter and Douglas R. Sease (1987) "Many Foreigners Find Building Plants Is Easier Than Making Money in U.S." *Wall Street Journal* (24 July):6.

Hagedorn, Ann (1987) "Campeau Won't Sell Allied's Ann Taylor and Brooks Brothers Chains, Sources Say." *Wall Street Journal* (23 February):4.

Hansard, Donna Steph (1988) "Just What Hath Campeau Wrought?" *Dallas Morning News* (19 June):H1+.

Helm, Leslie with Alice Z. Cuneo and Dean Foust (1988) "On the Campus: Fat Endowments and Growing Clout." *Business Week* (11 July):70+.

Herr, Ellen M. (1988) "U.S. Business Enterprises Acquired or Established by Foreign Direct Investors in 1987." *Survey of Current Business* 68(5):50-58.

Hirsch, Seev (1967) *Location of Industry and International Competitiveness.* New York: Oxford University Press.

Holstein, William J. with Amy Borrus (1988) "Japan's Clout in the U.S.: It's Translating Economic Might into Influence." *Business Week* (11 July):64–66.

Howenstine, Ned G. (1987) "U.S. Affiliates of Foreign Companies: Operations in 1985." *Survey of Current Business* 67(5):36–51.

Howes, Candace (1986) "U.S. Auto Jobs: The Problem is Bigger than Japanese Imports." *UAW Research Bulletin* (June):2–8.

Hymer, Stephen (1972) "The Multinational Corporation and the Law of Uneven Development." In *Economics and World Order from the 1970's to the 1990's*, edited by Jagdish N. Bhagwati, 113-40. New York: Macmillan.

Hymer, Stephen (1976) *The International Operations of National Firms: A Study of Direct Foreign Investment.* Cambridge, MA: MIT Press.

Hymowitz, Carol (1988) "Bloomingdale's May Reduce Staff by 400 as Parent Campeau Continues to Cut Costs." *Wall Street Journal* (8 June):5.

Japan Economic Journal Staff (1986) "Japanese Investments in the U.S. Are Riskier Than Many First Suppose." *Japan Economic Journal* (5 July):13+.

Keller, John J. with Mark Maremont (1987) "Plessey's New Face in the U.S." *Business Week* (20 April):32.

Kindleberger, Charles P. (1969) *American Business Abroad; Six Lectures on Direct Investment.* New Haven, CT: Yale University Press.

Koepp, Stephen (1987) "For Sale: America." *Time* 130(14 September):52–56+.

Malcolm, Andrew H. (1985) "Foreign Money Changing U.S. Social-Cultural Life." *New York Times* (31 December):1.

Mason, Todd and John Hoerr (1988) "Hitachi: Winning Friends and Influencing People in Oklahoma." *Business Week* (11 July):7–75.

New York Times Staff (1985) "Foreign Investment in U.S. Up Sharply." *New York Times* (16 September):D9.

Power, Christopher and Edith Terry (1986) "Now Campeau Has to Pay for His Pricey Prize." *Business Week* (17 November):66–67.

Prestowitz, Clyde V. (1988) *Trading Places: How We Allowed Japan to Take the Lead*. New York: Basic Books.

Reich, Robert B. (1988) "Corporation and Nation: What's Good for America's Largest Firms Is Not Necessarily Good for America." *Atlantic Monthly* 261 (May):76–81.

Rohatyn, Felix (1988) Address to the Economic Club of Washington, 26 January. Photocopy.

Rose, Robert L. and Ann Hagedorn (1987) "Carson Agrees to Acquire Unit of Allied Stores." *Wall Street Journal* (28 August):4.

Schoenberger, Erica (1986) "Multinational Corporations and the New International Division of Labor: Incorporating Competitive Strategies into a Theory of International Location." Baltimore: Department of Geography and Environmental Engineering, Johns Hopkins University.

Smick-Medley and Associates (1988) *Foreign Investment: A Smick-Medley and Associates Public Opinion Survey of U.S. Attitudes*. Washington, DC: Smick-Medley.

Teece, David J. (1985) "Multinational Enterprise, Internal Governance, and Industrial Organization." *American Economic Review* 75(2):233–38.

U.S. Bureau of the Census (1983) *1980 Benchmark Survey of Foreign Investment in the United States*. Washington, DC: Bureau of Economic Analysis.

U.S. Bureau of the Census (1984) *1980–81 Annual Survey of Manufactures*. Washington, DC: Bureau of the Census, U.S. Department of Commerce.

Vernon, Raymond (1966) "International Investment and International Trade in the Product Cycle." *Quarterly Journal of Economics* 80:190–207.

Vernon, Raymond (1971) *Sovereignty at Bay: The Multinational Spread of U.S. Enterprise*. New York: Basic Books.

Vernon, Raymond (1974) "The Location of Economic Activity." In *Economic Analysis and the Multinational Enterprise*, edited by John H. Dunning, 89-114. London: George Allen & Unwin.

COMMENT

James F. Smith

It is an honor to have been selected to discuss a paper co-authored by Professor Glickman. He is very highly regarded by all of us who have spent time toiling in the vineyards to produce econometric forecasts of states and metropolitan areas. During my time at Wharton Econometric Forecasting Associates (1985–86), we spent a lot of time building and refining models that were in all essential respects simply applications of his pioneering work on the Philadelphia model in 1969–70.

In the preceding chapter, Glickman and Woodward set out to discover the impact of foreign direct investment in the United States, particularly on the creation of employment opportunities for Americans. The beginning of the chapter suggests that foreign involvement in the U.S. economy may be unbelievably malign if it comes from another planet, but may possibly have some redeeming social virtues if investment simply comes from another country.

Glickman and Woodward provide a very lucid analysis of the growth in foreign direct investment in the United States over the past few years. There is very little for anyone to argue with in the initial sections of the chapter, which analyze the data, mostly from the Bureau of Economic Analysis of the U.S. Department of Commerce, covering 1982–86.

In analyzing the impact of foreign investment on job creation it is useful to remember that the BEA counts as foreign controlled any firm in which foreigners own a stake of 10 percent or more. This makes DuPont a foreign firm, because of the 22 percent stake held by Seagrams of Canada, and that alone distorts the numbers significantly.

Even with all the data limitations though, the bulk of the chapter documents that foreign investors haven't had an impact on the economy much different from that of the Fortune 500 over the 1982–86 period. Some firms have expanded, some have contracted, but the overall effect on jobs (and economic growth) has been small. As most of the authors in this book have said, the real engine of growth in the U.S. economy is small business and here, not surprisingly, foreign direct investment is a nonevent.

The chapter at best becomes highly controversial and, in my opinion, breaks down almost completely in the policy prescriptions and analysis at the end. The authors appear to have very little feel for American history. Virtually all job creation and economic growth in America came from foreigners from 1603–1783. The

103

vast majority of our participation in the industrial revolution was funded by foreigners and the United States did not reach a position where the value of our assets abroad was larger than foreigners' assets here until World War I devastated
the European economies.

The value of U.S. direct investment abroad still vastly exceeds the value of
foreign direct investment in this country and if we had any system for adjusting
book values to market values, this gap in favor of the United States would be far
above the published figures.

The bulk of Glickman and Woodward's policy prescriptions appear to have
come from the statements and platforms of Walter Mondale in 1980 or Michael
Dukakis in 1988, and the American public (or at least that minority that considers the benefits of voting to outweigh the costs) has resoundingly rejected these
views.

The facts are that the U.S. economy over the years since 1981 has created more
net new jobs (over 17 million) than any other economy in history. Furthermore,
we are the first $5 trillion economy (gross national product) in the history of the
world and while our share of world output has declined since World War II, it
was the same in 1988 as in 1938 and is still well over 25 percent.

The authors prescribe some kind of tripartite decision making on foreign investment by groups representing governments, business, and organized labor. Since
unionized workers are less than a fifth of the labor force and since most of their
new members in the last decade have been public employees, this gives two-thirds
of the power to government. It would be hard to devise a surer prescription for
disaster.

Glickman and Woodward scorn both laissez faire and free trade as "outmoded
concepts of little relevance to today's world." They seem to work very well for
Hong Kong, currently facing a 1.2 percent unemployment rate, and they remain
the best available policies for increasing standards of living, creating jobs, and
improving wealth ever devised by the minds of man. If Third World debtor nations would follow these policies, their citizens and their creditors would both be
much better off. Furthermore, the United States would regain the opportunity to
sell a great deal more goods and services to the countries that have historically
been among our largest export markets.

Of their six policy proposals, only one makes sense to anyone who understands
that free markets work to allocate resources in the most efficient manner. This is
their first proposal, which calls for gathering more and better data on foreign direct
investment. Indeed, the United States needs more and better data on capital flows,
trade flows, and almost all of the components of our national income and product accounts, not to mention industrial production and improved measures of
capacity.

Glickman and Woodward call for restoring U.S. international competitiveness.
Apparently, they have not noticed that manufacturing productivity has grown 4.2
percent a year since 1980, the highest rate for any comparable period since World
War II. They also seem to have missed the Office of the Organization for Eco-

nomic Cooperation and Development (OECD) report that shows the U.S..taxes on corpo rate profits to be lower than in any other OECD country, making the United States extremely attractive to both foreign and domestic producers. And the growth rate for U.S. exports in 1987–89 has been exceeded in the postwar period only by 1947–49.

Their third policy proposal is to raise taxes and reduce the trade deficit. This, of course, was exactly the policy course followed by the Hoover Administration, with disastrous consequences for the U.S. and world economies. The U.S. needs drastically to reduce the rate of increase in federal government spending in defense and nondefense, but the last thing America needs is more taxes. Indeed, total tax revenues have soared as tax rates have been reduced from confiscatory to merely annoying levels.

U.S. antitrust policies are already much more stringent than in most of our major competitor nations. They need to be enforced fairly against domestic and foreign companies, but we don't need any more such laws and we certainly don't need more laws to increase the powers of entrenched managers over shareholders.

Their fifth policy proposal is to reduce competition among states and localities for foreign investment. Since these entities compete for domestic plants (and government projects) even harder, this policy cannot succeed. There is very little evidence that incentives make much difference in the vast majority of decisions anyway. Petrochemical industry investment will go to Texas and Louisiana while tobacco industry investment will go to Kentucky, North Carolina, or Virginia regardless of incentives.

The Glickman and Woodward policy proposals on plant closings would have the United States copy France and West Germany. If you make it hard enough to fire people, you'll eventually discover a very high unemployment rate because employers won't hire people in the first place.

The authors have a few comments about companies and their "commitments" to their headquarters countries that no finance professor can pass up. The company that forgets that its primary responsibility is to make money for its shareholders is a perfect candidate for a takeover or leveraged buy out.

The very end of the chapter contains a most important point that should have been developed in greater detail. Glickman and Woodward point out that capital shifts much more quickly than either workers or communities, which tend to move only in California. A strong government program to retrain workers who don't want to move, and to provide assistance to communities in diversifying their economies, such as the phenomenally successful adjustments for almost every military base closed in the 1960s and early 1970s, would certainly be a far better use of the taxpayer's money than many existing programs.

In summary, this chapter contains an excellent analysis of the (very small) impact of foreign direct investment on the U.S. economy and total employment picture. The chapter would have been much better if it had stopped with that and left the highly interventionist, mostly unrelated, and extremely controversial policy proposals out altogether.

5 JOB CREATION, BUSINESS GROWTH, AND STATE POLICY: GLIMPSES OF THE THIRD WAVE

Robert E. Friedman

Jobs and business growth have always been the immediate objects of state economic development, but our understanding of their dynamics and the policy initiatives appropriate to spur them has changed markedly. It is possible to discuss these relatively distinct waves in that development policy—the first in the mid-1930s, the next some 30 to 40 years later.

THE FIRST AND SECOND WAVES

For all intents and purposes, the first wave of modern state economic development policy began in 1936 when Mississippi launched its Balance Agriculture with Industry (BAWI) program. The strategy was straightforward: lure manufacturing branch plants (new and existing) from the high-cost North by marketing the low costs of labor, land, government, and living in Mississippi. And if costs were not low enough, BAWI would reduce them further through government subsidy parading in any number of forms from tax abatements, to customized training, to outright grants.

It worked. For a while. Employment rolls and wages rose dramatically relative to the rest of the country during the 1950s, and more modestly in the 1960s. The strategy spread, of course in the Southeast, but also increasingly, to all corners of the country, from New Hampshire to Washington, to Arizona. If the existing private costs of doing business weren't low enough, then there were always taxes to credit or abate, subsidized loans to offer.

107

By the late 1970s, and clearly in the early 1980s the strategy was producing ever more limited results in the South. Fewer plants were coming; more were closing or leaving the country for cheaper territory. The march of per capita incomes toward the national average slowed, stopped, and some places even reversed.

The second wave of state development policy began not in the South, but in New England in the early and mid-1970s. Here the first impact of global economic restructuring was first felt, most directly in the acute contraction of the apparel and footwear industries.

After some initial flailing at stopping the closings (a chase pursued longer, if unsuccessfully, at the federal level), states discovered the growing strength of new, young, and small businesses, often (not always) in information and service industries. Even before David Birch and others taught them how to count the job and growth contribution of such firms, Massachusetts and other states like Connecticut, California, and Minnesota began to craft policies aimed at stimulating and steering the growth of such firms. Massachusetts spewed out a stream of quasi-public financial institutions aimed at plugging perceived capital market gaps; built roads, targeted state aid, and laid a foundation of community-based development organizations to stimulate development in depressed communities; launched a series of training, retraining, and employment-linking programs; created new joint university-business research and technology transfer programs.

The second wave spread, first to other states in New England, then to states like California, Minnesota, Colorado, and Washington, feeling the initial impact of global competition from East and West alike. In general the innovation would follow the onslaught of global restructuring. It traveled to the industrial heartland, where leaner, more modern Japanese and German manufacturers would move in on the markets of Midwest automobile and steel firms in the mid-1970s. Many of these states—notably Michigan, Ohio, Pennsylvania, Illinois, and Indiana—would respond with an array of new financing, technology, training, infrastructure initiatives, and labor-management cooperation initiatives, often adapting programs as they adopted them, to reflect lessons learned from the Northeast experience and the industrial nature of the midwestern economy.

In the late 1970s and early 1980s, it was the Southeast's turn, as underdeveloped Third World countries opened their doors to firms seeking cheaper homes for a more mobile capital and technology. The South awoke to find the bill come due from its earlier Faustian bargain of short-term industrial gains at the expense of long-term investments in the people, businesses, and infrastructures of their states. But, if the challenge of 100 years of poverty and 50 of underinvestment were huge, Southern leaders didn't blink. Led by states like Florida and North Carolina, later Arkansas, South Carolina, and the new Mississippi, the South was the first region to realize fully the centrality of educational investment and reform to economic development, a reality which spread to other sections of the country.

The collapse of resource industries—agriculture, mining, energy—in the early 1980s plunged the high-flying economies of the Plains and Mountain states from

Texas to Alaska into duress. Some states—Oklahoma and Iowa, notably—have used second-wave policies to reverse their fortunes, evolving creative rural strategies. But most of these states have yet to respond.

The Northeast, of course, is back—at least if one considers unemployment rates, income, and trade measures. The Midwest is coming back, led by leaner, more technologically advanced and more flexible manufacturing firms. And the South, while still hobbled by the time it takes for investments in basic foundations of growth to mature, shows rising business prowess. And throughout the period we have been adding 600 thousand firms and 2 million jobs annually.

Policy had something to do with it. How much is a matter of debate. Policy probably added only incrementally and on the margins over a long period of time. But the pattern of recovery is too consistent, the results too tangible, for the message not to be clear: investing in yourself pays.

THE POLICY FRAMEWORK

Five years ago, after about five years of toiling in the policy vineyards of state and local government, we at the Corporation for Enterprise Development decided to take a step back, and attempt to understand better the dynamics of today's economy, and the strategies likely to yield success. We reviewed virtually every major study we could find on the foundations of long-term, widely shared economic health, the nature of the global economy, the dynamics of job and business growth, and the programs, policies, and practices with the most evidence of success. We examined our own experience working with states and communities, here and abroad. After broad consultation, we constructed the index and subindex structure of the Development Report Card for the States—hereafter called the Report Card. We looked for the best measures we could find to illuminate how states were doing relative to one another on those diverse dimensions of economic health. In 1989, we issued our third edition, now with 125 measures as well as international benchmarks (see Corporation for Enterprise Development, 1987, 1988, 1989).

The Report Card is not a precise, econometric model. A good deal of subjective judgment went into it. It is at best a first-order and impressionistic diagnostic tool.

That said, the framework has withstood the very public scrutiny of economists, business and labor leaders, state officials, the press, and community leaders. And its acceptance grows—in high-performing states and low. We continue to believe that the Report Card framework coheres better with what we know about economic development than any other index available.

But the real test, and the one I am most comfortable with is yours. Does it make sense to you, given the sum of your experience and knowledge?

The Report Card is premised on the understanding that we will no longer compete in this world economy with any real opportunity of offering our people chances of a better standard of living on a pure cost basis. We will not be, whether we are in Michigan or Mississippi, the lowest cost place to do business in the globe. If all you really need as a business is simply a low-cost environment—unskilled labor, cheap machinery, no taxes, no education system—there will be cheaper places to do business in the Third World countries. I don't think we want to be a Third World country.

The Report Card asks four basic questions to assess the long-term health of a state economy. The same questions apply at the community level, the national level, the international level.

1. *Economic performance*. How well is the economy performing in terms of its primary purpose of providing the citizens of the state and their children with chances for a better life?

2. *Business vitality*. How competitive are existing businesses in the state? At what rate and how broadly are new businesses being formed?

3. *Resource capacity*. Are the resources in place to fuel future growth and start-ups?

4. *Public policy*. Is the public sector an active and intelligent partner with the private sector in making sure that basic investments and basic service are in place?

Economic Performance

The Report Card asks four kinds of questions about economic performance.

1. *Employment*. How available are jobs? Can all who want one get one? What's the rate of new job formation? What's the duration of unemployment?

2. *Job quality*. How much do jobs pay? What benefits like health coverage do they carry? After all, not all jobs are created equal. Here we clearly depart from traditional thinking. Traditionalists would say the higher your wages are the worse a place you are to do business. But to us, high wages, and rising per capita income, are primary goals of economic development. The trick and the challenge is to make sure that *productivity increases faster than income*, to find ways of adding value so that you can justify a continually improving quality of life.

3. *Equity*. How widely is prosperity shared around in the state?

4. *Quality of life*. What is the quality of life related to this economy? We recognize that people don't live by bread alone.

Business Vitality

We think business development is a means to an end, not an end in itself; but it is the primary means to the end. In this business vitality index, we look primarily at the health, growth, and formation of in-state businesses. This is not to say that you don't look outside, that you don't recruit. However, this index is based on several findings from the best research in the area that indicate that the private sources of economic strength come from businesses within states.

First, in most states during the last 15 years, at least 80 percent of new jobs have come from businesses that start up or expand within the state. And that's a conservative figure. The lion's share of new jobs are coming from inside. It means to me that that's the dog and recruitment is the tail, which should primarily assist and complement.

Second, what does it take to be competitive in today's global economy? To find the answer, we think it best to look at businesses that are doing very well in this economy. An association of such businesses in Washington, the American Business Conference (ABC), claims to be the only meritocracy in Washington; it may well be. The ABC membership is about 100 firms representing all sectors of the economy—high tech, low tech, manufacturing, service, financial, and real estate. These companies, by any standard, are winners in the global competition. They have on average, increased their earnings from international sales 20 percent a year in the 1980s—five times the national average. They have increased employment on an average each year of 14 percent.

ABC surveyed its members and asked "How are you competing?" The answers were very clear. They were all competing in terms of quality, service, innovation, flexibility, timeliness—not cost. In fact, they said they couldn't afford to pay their people low wages, because they needed not just their brawn; they needed their brains.

True, again, across sectors. We're not just talking service here; we're not just talking manufacturing.

When the ABC firms were asked "What do you need?" they didn't refer to the absence of things. The two items topping their agenda were (1) a good education system (and a skilled and adaptable labor force) and (2) access to capital at the right times and of the right kinds.

Third, what you find when you examine scientific studies of the determinants of business location decisions, is that location is idiosyncratic. But if you look at the preponderance of answers, they're always the same things: quality of the labor force, quality of the education system, quality of life, proximity to growing markets. Way down the list come cost factors.

I'm not saying you should ignore costs; obviously you would want to keep costs to a minimum. But often you get what you pay for, whether it's labor, skills, adaptability, and commitment, or quality of the raw materials. Interestingly enough, 30 percent of the cost of a manufactured good now, in general, in the United States, is a function of poor quality—the cost of rejects, repair, inspection. Most companies that have focused on quality end up not only achieving increased quality but drastically reduced costs.

My point is that this is a case where you can have your cake and eat it, too. Do the things that are necessary to grow in-state business—develop the education system, the quality of life, a flexible and adaptable labor force, good infrastructure—and you also have a very attractive environment for out-of-state plants.

The only danger in recruitment seems to me to be if it becomes the sole focus or is pursued in such a way, as I think it too often was in some southern states, that it undermines in-state investments. I find it very significant that two years ago a candidate for governor won an election by running against a Toyota plant incentive package which was thought to be too large and unfair to in-state businesses and in-state citizens.

Competitiveness of existing business. To assess competitiveness we look at manufacturing investment rates, business failure rates, traded sector strength.

Entrepreneurial energy. We look at entrepreneurial energy—the rate at which businesses are forming and the breadth of new business formation. Our best data suggest that over the last 15 years, half of new jobs created in any community and in any state of the union came from independent firms under five years of age. That means that if the next 5 years are at all like the past 15, half the new jobs created in the United States in the year 1994 will be created by businesses that don't now exist, by people not now in business but who are overwhelmingly already resident in the state.

It means if you focus only on existing businesses, you almost by definition miss at least half of the target. It means to me that you've got to look beyond existing businesses to invest in people and the infrastructure and those unidentifiable entrepreneurs who will create the business and identify the markets of tomorrow.

We watch business formation rates, the percentage of companies that are growing very rapidly. We also look at the breadth of business formation—the rates of women's and minority business ownership, controlling for labor force participation. Not as an equity measure (although it is) but as a vitality measure. Nationally, the rate of women's business formation is now increasing at three to five times that of men's. Women's business formation is an incredible resource, it seems to me, to be drawn upon. It is also, I might add, our secret weapon against the Japanese, who have not realized that their own women have any economic role to play.

Economic diversity. We also consider the diversity of the economy—the extent to which the economy not only looks diverse but acts diverse.

Resource Capacity

Are the resources in place to fuel continued growth? What are those resources?

Human resources. Far and away, all the evidence we have suggests that the key resource is the human resource. Edward Dennison at the Brookings Institution figures he can account for 75 percent of gross national product (GNP) growth in this country over the last 50 years through increases in human capital—the health, use, and skills of the labor force. And everything we know suggests that human skills only become more important from here on out. The Workforce 2000

Report for the Department of Labor (Hudson Institute, 1987) suggests that by the year 2000, half of new jobs will require college-level skills. On average in this country, a little more than 20 percent of the labor force has college-level skills.

Technology resources. We then look at technology resources—fundamentally another form of human resources. We look at things like numbers of scientists and engineers, federal research and development (R&D), university R&D, and patent rates.

Financial capacity. We consider financial capacity. Not just how much a state has, but whether it's accessible to growing business. We look at the availability of seed capital for start-ups, venture capital or other sorts of risk capital, and debt money for business expansions.

Physical resources, infrastructure and amenities. Finally, we examine the traditional infrastructure—roads, sewers; the new infrastructure of telecommunications (we don't have a good measure for it but we at least ask the question); plus availability and cost of housing (controlled for per capita income), environmental amenities, environmental qualities, arts, and doctors.

Public Policy

Finally, we look at public policy. The traditional myth is that the best government is the one that governs least, that all you have to do for the economy to prosper is to get government out. But when we looked around at the states that continually seemed to perform well in terms of employment, income, patents, and so on, they were states like Massachusetts, Connecticut, Minnesota, and California. These states have a strong public sector working together with a strong private sector, making sure that the basic investments in education and infrastructure and the basic services—police, fire, whatever—were in place. Private investment depends on those services and those investments. There are things the private sector won't do, can't do on its own such as basic education, basic literacy. It is no accident, it seems to me, that it is business that has led the push for increased investment in education in Texas, in Washington, in Colorado, even at the expense of higher taxes, because business has to pay the bill for an undereducated and underskilled labor force.

We look at six areas of public policy because we think the time is long past when economic development was something that only the department of economic development or the development board or the department of commerce did.

Tax structure. We study tax structure, not tax level. Taxes may be too high or too low; but the issue really is, Are you getting what you pay for? And we found no way of measuring that directly. One of my favorite editorials after we came out with the first Report Card in 1987 appeared in the *Atlanta Constitution*. Its theme was "you get what you pay for." In part, it said:

> For generations, especially in the South, three little words have served as a talisman
> for politicians: no new taxes. The last fellow to invoke them in the face of likely

defeat was 1982 gubernatorial candidate Joe Frank Harris. He won. The truth is, though, this potion loses its magic quickly as users set about to bolster state economies.

We look directly at tax structure. Business investments are long-term investments; to that extent they depend on a predictable level of public investment and public services. Businesses want to know year-in, year-out whether those services and investments are going to be around. We looked at the balance and stability of the tax system. Could the tax system, in good years and in bad, in recession and expansion, produce the revenues necessary to underwrite the essential services and investments? A big problem in Louisiana, Texas, and Alaska right now is that they built their entire tax structure on petroleum revenues, and they're in trouble.

We also consider the fairness of the tax system—across industry lines, income groups, and communities. Taxes should not determine the investment decision. What we want is lots of people making decisions about what they think are the best investments based on underlying value and on their expectations of future return.

Capital mobilization. We look at mobilizing capital. Most investments for business development will come from the private sector. The question here is not direct public investments, although, sometimes that's needed. The question is to what extent is the public sector working with private financial institutions to adjust to the new economy where risk is inevitable and opportunity is abundant but where you have to be not risk-avoiders but risk-managers. There are many cheap ways to do that.

Education. We investigate the level of support for education, for while you don't always get what you pay for, you rarely get more than you pay for. We also look at reform efforts to insure and increase the maximum impact for the expenditure.

Business and technical assistance. We look at business and technical assistance. Is technology getting out of the labs into commerce? Are there incubator programs in place? Are small business assistance centers available? States are already involved in many of these techniques.

Infrastructure. We examine the extent to which a state knows its infrastructure needs and assesses them regularly; we examine investments in affordable housing, environmental quality, and health care.

Investment in distressed communities. Finally, we look at investment in distressed communities, for instance, at the transfer payments system, particularly welfare and unemployment compensation.

Having a safety net makes people willing to take risks—it enables them and it conserves human resources. But those payments can do more than merely maintain; they can become investments in economic independence and employment and job creation. We measure the extent to which states invest transfer payments in this way.

We also look at community development corporation programs. State government is often like a centipede without legs; the legs—community institutions like community development corporations and neighborhood development organizations—are absolutely crucial. We need to develop those legs.

THE SECOND WAVE: ACHIEVEMENTS AND LIMITS

The achievements of the second wave are significant. Much has been tried, much has been learned, and a pattern of recovery has emerged which is hard to separate totally from the new policies.

But the limits of the second wave are becoming equally clear. First are the unabated challenges apparent in the pattern of results of the 1989 Development Report Card for the States: growing income inequality in virtually every state (only Hawaii, Alaska, and North Dakota broke the pattern) and the nation as a whole; acute distress in rural states (12 of the 13 states receiving no grade higher than a C on any index, are best described as rural) and rural areas of states. Growth and development are simply not reaching all areas of the country.

The second limit, also noted in the Report Card's international measures, is the sense that whatever the success of second-wave policy, we are not yet meeting the test of international competitiveness. While we have responded to the impacts of international competition, we continue to lag behind our major trading partners on such measures as income growth, productivity improvement, exports and trade, and manufacturing equipment investment. Our businesses are doubly buffered from meeting international standards—by the size of our domestic market and by the lower standards of the most visible, domestic competitors. Having observed whole regions of Europe where virtually every business operates at global standards—tracking global market trends, using the new technologies, employing broadly trained workers as partners in defining production, always seeking to improve quality—I fear that most American businesses simply do not yet understand the nature of the competition they face (any more than do most students and schools). When the National Federation of Independent Business (NFIB) surveyed its 500 thousand small-firm members last year, they ranked exporting as 75th out of 75 problems they faced; it wasn't a problem because they didn't do it. That leaves a great problem for the nation. It is a challenge not only of magnitude, but time: How long do we have before the gap between general business practice, or general education practice, becomes so wide that catching up becomes unreasonable? I would guess the period is measured in years, not decades.

The third limit is the piecemeal approach to development. The current state of second-wave strategies reflects a piecemeal approach to development. Existing practice generally compartmentalizes development initiatives so that the services are not delivered in a manner sensitive to the total needs of a business or community, but instead provides separate, often uncoordinated assistance for technology needs, financing needs, training needs, et cetera. Program developers view the needs of the business or community through the narrow perspective of what their program can offer rather than what the client needs. It is not unusual for a training program, for instance, to see all problems as training problems.

Also, the actors involved in economic development are often kept apart. Economic development is increasingly everybody's business—chambers of commerce, universities, nonprofits, government agencies, school boards, and so on. And tackling the complex obstacles that constrain our development potential, from inadequate labor force skills to insufficient investment in new R&D, entails the creation of more and better public/private/nonprofit partnerships, where each actor is positioned to what it does best.

A fourth limit is the lack of integration of social and economic policy. Social problems need economic solutions and the key to a revitalized economy is to bring new people and products to the marketplace. Keeping our efforts bifurcated perpetuates a vicious circle of a faltering economy blocking further social programs, while increasing rates of poverty, crime, ill health, and poor education undermine our economic dynamism.

The fifth limit is the lack of accountability. The most fitting characteristic describing the shift to a "home-grown" economic development strategy is broad experimentation. States across the nation have been trying to uncover ways of promoting and sustaining economic growth among their existing and newly formed businesses. But experimentation too often placed an emphasis on innovation at the neglect of evaluation. At the end of nearly a decade of this second wave, there is a paucity of indicators to measure the successes and failures of the approaches undertaken. This lack of performance data makes it difficult to refine or adapt these newly crafted initiatives—that is, to learn from the experiences of them.

A related concern is that many of the initiatives created during this period of experimentation failed to articulate clearly who their intended clientele were and why. And even those initiatives that set clear and reasonable eligibility standards often neglected ways to promote ownership of these initiatives by their intended clientele and to require a client investment in the services being offered. By not emphasizing a client-matching investment of some sort, these initiatives missed an opportunity to create an automatic and self-enforcing feedback loop into the desirability and value of their services.

Finally, and most fundamentally, second-wave policies beg the question of scale. Even if you accept the general proposition that the theoretical and empirical evidence suggests that policy has had something to do with the pattern of state recovery from international shocks, especially when measured against the magnitude of the domestic and international challenges we face, the question becomes, is it enough?

Thus far, I think the answer has to be no. All the educational reform and investment efforts of the past five years have yielded improvements of about 5 percent in test scores; still the educational system fails on the order of 30 percent of the kids going through it—kids who don't finish, let alone the ones who do with little to show. Most of the hundred or so development finance programs launched by states in the last decade are lucky if they supply (needed) capital to a handful of businesses; in no way do they generally change the overall availability of capital in state economies. Rural and urban areas alike remain mired in new and historic disadvantage. Business assistance programs reach out to few businesses with advice of uneven quality.

In reality the challenges are one and overlapping. We cannot maintain a globally competitive economy if we are doomed to carry one-third of the nation in dependency. And however laudatory the results of program and policy initiatives, if they are too small or too slow to induce the needed change, then there is little cause for satisfaction.

The question becomes, Are the policies of the magnitude of the challenges and opportunities we face? If not, we must take what we have learned from second-wave policies to craft a more adequate new generation of policy—the third wave. We can begin to discern some of the dimensions of the third wave by looking at some emerging policies and policy proposals.

GLIMPSES OF THE THIRD WAVE

Education

That American education is not producing students educated to the skill levels required to meet current requirements, let alone the demands of global competitiveness, is not news. The statistics are now fairly familiar: one-third of ninth-graders drop out before completing high school. Most high school graduates fail to meet levels of math, science, geography, even reading competency achieved by students in Singapore and other trading partners; we instead pride ourselves in the fact that 95 percent exceed sixth-grade competency standards. Skill bottlenecks show up with increasing frequency, stifling our most booming state economies, condemning lagging economies to further mediocrity (see Brizius, 1989, and related articles in the same issue of *The Entrepreneurial Economy Review.*)

And so most states have mounted education improvements efforts, at once increasing funding and introducing various reforms. But this wave of reforms has consisted chiefly in getting more out of the current system by increasing accountability, setting minimum standards for graduation rates and so on, raising teacher certification and testing requirements, improving school management, and introducing special programs for particular groups of students. The results have been predictably modest: the best data we have suggest improvements of no more than 5 percent over several years in increased student competency.

The realization is dawning that we cannot get dramatically different results by pushing the existing machine a little harder, greasing it a little more. Instead, we will have to change fundamentally how we educate. The third-wave reforms necessary to do this are beginning to emerge:

1. Move from a "batch process" means of educating, where students are grouped in classes and taught the same things en masse, to individualized, computer-based instruction.

2. Treat schools as the unit of reform, allowing parents, teachers, and students under the leadership of the principal wide discretion for producing better results, rewarding improvements with large financial incentives which in turn can power further innovation.

3. Extend the school year (Japanese students train year-round), and the school day; implement early childhood education and after-school programs everywhere.

4. Adopt a "zero defects" goal, just like modern industry.

South Carolina has produced marked improvements from a school-based incentive program. And school districts as diverse as those in Miami, Harlem, and Rochester have been able to show results from more entrepreneurial systems.

Development Finance

Most states' development finance programs provide subsidized loans directly to a few worthy businesses. Even if we assume for a minute that all those deals are good and necessary—surely a heroic assumption given the loss rates, allegations of political interference, and so forth experienced—they are not even conceivably of a magnitude to change the overall performance of a state economy. After all, in most states we are dealing with hundreds of thousands of businesses, and financial investment in the tens of billions. A state is unlikely to appropriate much more than $10–20 million to establish a development bank (see Hansen, 1988).

But if the resources committed are modest, the gaps they seek to fill are huge such as lack of seed and risk capital, expansion debt. The best evidence we have is that capital is most difficult to obtain precisely when it is most needed for growth. For example, when NFIB polled its members to see how well banks were meeting their credit needs, the overall response, 94–95 percent, was "just fine"; but the 4–5 percent who said their credit needs weren't being met were the ones who were growing, whose credit and needs this year were different from credit needs last year. The challenge is really to change private-sector investment behavior—individual and institutional.

The Michigan Strategic Fund (MSF) is the one development finance institution in the country that at least attempts to take on the task of changing financial behavior/culture (see Plastrik and Rohde, 1988). The principles underlying its four innovative windows are instructive.

1. *Extend financing at market rates.* The primary issue is access to capital, not cost. Market rate financing helps reduce substitution of public for private capital and allows the MSF to achieve long-term sustainability, even growth.

2. *Target financing to identified market gaps.* The MSF's windows are aimed

at providing seed capital, mezzanine risk capital, expansion debt, and capital to minority ventures.

3. *Wholesale capital to privately managed institutions.* By investing state funds in privately managed institutions meeting the purposes of the program, Michigan avoids political influence on investments and the difficulty of attracting, maintaining, and managing highly specialized, skilled, and expensive personnel. It can also move more money and leverage more.

4. *Leverage private capital.* By requiring a private-sector matching investment, Michigan introduces a market test of the desirability of the financing vehicle and multiplies the impact of the state investment. Direct leverage ratios—the ratio of total funds in the pool to public contributions—runs from a minimum of 2:1, to a high of 17:1 in the Capital Access Program.

The MSF has only been operating for a little more than a year, so it is too early to call it a success. But already it has induced the participating of 60 banks and 160 businesses in the Capital Access (expansion debt) Program; set up six BIDCO's (business and industrial development companies) expected to provide $500 million in mezzanine financing over a decade; created a pool of $10 million in seed capital; and established several new seed funds.

Human Investment

If, indeed, investment in yourself pays, then perhaps the problem in the chronically depressed communities not sharing in general recovery is that we haven't included them in the investment strategy. Oversimplified, the argument becomes this: for 50 years we have *spent* on the poor, but we haven't *invested* in them. Indeed, our transfer payment programs (welfare, unemployment compensation, social security) have been premised on the social contract that says to the needy, We will support you as long as you don't seek training, you don't work, and you don't, of all things, try to create a job for yourself. Pursue any of these routes to economic independence, and we will reduce benefits, often precipitously. The predictable result of such a contract is that effort is penalized, and the poor are separated and stigmatized. Money is spent, but the returns—economic and political—are limited to sustained consumption.

Another way is Transfer Payment Investment (TPI); it asks how existing transfer programs can be changed to encourage and support individual (and group) movement toward economic independence through social support, skill development, employment, and self-employment. The opening moves of this change are already in evidence—in the extension of medical coverage and child care to welfare recipients moving into the work force contained in last year's welfare reform bill, and in the broadened range of choices and state investments contained in programs like Massachusetts' Employment and Training Choices program. But it is perhaps best signalled by the experiments underway in a dozen states to open a realistic self-employment option to the poor and unemployed (see Friedman, 1988).

During the last eight years, 12 other nations have changed their unemployment compensation and welfare systems to allow unemployed people receiving benefits to continue receiving benefits, sometimes in a lump sum, if they want to try to create a job for themselves. The most reliable data come from the British Enterprise Allowance Scheme which has let more than 500 thousand unemployed people—2–3 percent of those eligible— start a business. Even though little business assistance is provided, 54 percent of the businesses are still trading and profitable three years after start-up. The businesses are creating an average of one and a half to two jobs each, and the British Exchequer figures that after the third year of the program, it actually makes money on the scheme.

The state experiments now under way test whether we can achieve such results in the United States with its far more varied unemployed and disadvantaged population. It is too early to know how well these experiments will work, but we are already finding some interesting things.

1. The response among welfare recipients and unemployed people to the option is extraordinary. Three hundred people showed up to an introductory meeting in Detroit; 140 people called in within 36 hours of hearing about the program in Meridian, Mississippi.

2. Many long-term welfare recipients will opt for the program.

3. Already successful businesses have been started up by welfare recipients and dislocated workers.

But perhaps the real benefit of the program is not so much the 1 or 2 percent of dependent people it will help to escape poverty, but rather the changes in thinking it induces. First, in this age of the entrepreneur, if the public comes to understand that welfare recipients are not only potential clients, beneficiaries, trainees, and employees, but also potential entrepreneurs and creators of wealth, it has to take another look at who is poor and why they are poor and what the ways out of poverty might be. In short, people begin to recognize that the capacity to produce exists and justifies efforts to expand it. In so doing a social and political trust can increase. Second, it can help us see the benefits of changing a maintenance system into an investment system. If, like the British, we find out that, in fact, our willingness to invest some money today will produce greater returns in the future, then we have a powerful, political as well as economical program. This scenario begins to suggest the outlines of a much broader human investment strategy.

For almost 50 years we have had one set of policies to guard the mainstream health of the economy—largely a domain of white men—and another for social service—those who cannot support themselves in the mainstream economy—largely women and minorities. The limits of that bifurcated system are now obvious; while the rising tide helps, it does not lift all boats. Meanwhile, the maintenance of social service systems may have provided a net but no ladder. A human investment system would bridge and integrate this bifurcated structure. It would say to people, "We will invest in you and in your efforts at economic improvement, if you will invest yourself—your talent, your efforts, your resources." Note that money would be invested only where individuals are willing themselves to invest; and in that sense the entitlement is earned. Money would be dispersed according to return on investments. This is a strategy to increase supply, not simply to distribute it, by engaging, building, harnessing the productive capacity of people's energy and vision. It is designed to produce returns greater than the initial investment. We have good evidence and have many social programs—Head Start is the clearest example—where returns exceed investment, though we have never attempted in a coherent way to invest discretionary public funds on the basis of return, or to develop accounting and monitoring that would track real returns on investment. Of course, this is something we can never do perfectly and we can only do it inadequately at present, but we can certainly do better than we do now, and in building a system to collect the numbers and quantify returns, we build a powerful political and economic rationale for increased investment and increased returns over time.

People get poor for different reasons and they will escape through different routes. A human investment system can accommodate the wide range of choices of routes to self-sufficiency—training, education, employment, and self-employment. And it can do so in a way that builds political and economic strengths over time. The outlines of the approach are clear enough; the precedents are mounting. But no state has yet to launch a truly integrated human investment system. It would not be outrageously difficult to do this; in its initial stages it could be done simply by reprogramming existing funds.

Business Assistance

Most states and localities provide assistance to business the old-fashioned way—one-to-one, one-by-one—that is, one (public or nonprofit) technical assistance provider to one business person. It is an expensive system and a slow one where no adequate evidence exists of the general effectiveness of the approach as a whole and where clearly the effectiveness of individual assistance providers varies dramatically. Most importantly it is clearly not of the scale of the challenge in terms of extent of business effect, or speed.

The challenges indeed are huge. The problem, it seems to me, is not so much a problem of our best businesses. The top 5 or 10 percent of American businesses—large and small, young and old, manufacturing and service—are probably as competitive as any in the world. They meet global standards of awareness of global market trends, application of the new technologies, broad training of the employees in diverse skills, new management techniques that treat workers as partners and potential entrepreneurs. The best evidence we have is that the next 90 percent are not so operating. Yet, clearly in other countries, and certainly other regions of countries like Italy, Germany, Denmark, and Sweden, virtually every business, however small, including microbusinesses, operate at global standards.

The way these other countries and regions have accomplished this change in business culture is instructive. In these "network regions" large numbers of small businesses collaborate to accomplish together what they cannot accomplish alone: tracking market trends, investigating new technology, purchasing new technology, negotiating working capital loans, developing design talent (Friedman, 1987; see related articles in the same issue of *The Entrepreneurial Economy*). Sometimes seeded by government, these collaborative activities grow out of institutionalized communication among the firms which means that almost the moment any firm identifies a new market trend, or technological adaptation, all the firms in the region know about it. In essence, instead of trainers or assistance providers training firms, the firms teach and learn from one another. It is a more proven and respected source of advice.

The most noted network region, though by no means the only one in Italy, let alone in the rest of Europe, is the state-size region of Emilia-Romagna, just north of Florence, south of Venice, and east of the heavy industrial area of Milan and Turin. This region of four million people climbed from 17th among Italy's 30 regions in per capita income to 2nd in a 10-year period as wages rose from 90 percent—the Italian norm—to 125 percent. They accomplished this remarkable increase through the sort of networking described above. They did it in many small steps, not through any one breakthrough. They built on the base they had, on the people they had. In this region in Italy, there are now 325 thousand businesses, one for every five members of the active labor force of 1.7 million. In this region, 3 of 10 workers start businesses each year. When you go to the technical schools, kids describe their career path as "mastering the trade, working in a small firm, starting my own" (Hatch, 1987).

There are examples of networks in the United States. It is no accident perhaps that the industry which best demonstrates this form of organization is the film industry with its high-quality standards, rapidly evolving technology, and high needs for creativity. But conscious experimentation is only beginning.

At their best, network models suggest a very different and promising way of upgrading and modernizing business culture. In many ways it is the business assistance analog of the Michigan Strategic Fund. It is a process which allow states to wholesale business assistance by engaging the efforts of firms to help one another and in that way leverage private-sector funds to the purpose at hand. It overcomes, as well, what we have noticed as a chief limit of many of our capital assistance, managerial assistance, technology transfer programs: there may be need but there is no appetite. When we think of modernization in this country we have generally provided one of those three things—capital, managerial assistance, technology. In Europe, the order is reversed and preceded by a focus on global market trends and product design efforts. By focusing on those opportunities, businesses can see more clearly the bottom line benefits of modernization; the inquiries whet the appetite for the other innovations and create a private-sector demand so great that the private sector is indeed willing to finance the collaborative projects itself. Indeed, we know there are service centers to provide collaborative services in Europe that started with public funding and are now 95 percent supported by private-sector funds.

Entrepreneurial Systems

We are beginning to learn that how we do things is just as important as what we do. When you look closely at the models above that suggest the nature of a third wave, there are some common elements of how they operate that may not be coincidental. Indeed, they all seem to exhibit elements of what we might call *entrepreneurial systems*:

1. Desired outcomes are clear and measurable. The return on investment criteria for the human investment system and the educational improvement measures are clear.

2. Many actors are engaged and encouraged to take initiative. All of these systems—educational, human investment, financial, business assistance—encourage new actors—private, nonprofit, public—to get involved and do business in new ways.

3. They are investment systems premised on a show of effort by welfare recipient, school, student, or business, where private-sector effort is matched by public investment.

4. They provide information to a broad number of actors. Good information is a prerequisite for an operating market. Most of these systems generate information. In fact, monitoring becomes a crucial part of these systems. New measurement systems that provide real-time feedback on the effectiveness of programs according to their purposes is essential. Those new information systems are beginning to emerge. For example, Arizona, Florida, and other states are requiring vocational education operators to report the social security numbers of their students which they then run against the covered employment files to find placement rates and income levels which are later published—providing signals to students, administrators, and parents. Similar information systems are an integral part of educational reform efforts and the human investment systems.

5. Perhaps most importantly, all the systems allow the many actors greater discretion on how to accomplish the goals while holding them accountable for results. Thus, educational reform efforts give schools greater freedom to figure out how to achieve results; the human investment system similarly avails welfare recipients of diverse choices.

We need to recognize entrepreneurship as an attribute not just of the private sector in terms of small firm formation, but also as a characteristic that can apply to larger firms, the nonprofit sector, and indeed the public sector. The best definition of entrepreneurship seems to me to be the process of combining resources and new ways to add value. There is a premium on constantly figuring out how to do things better and differently. It means that all our systems must become more entrepreneurial—that all our institutions must become more entrepreneurial. Thus, how the system is structured, the spread of entrepreneurial systems to all aspects of policy becomes more than a question of means; it becomes the key, we think, to unlocking the challenge of scale.

Obviously, we can only glimpse the emergence of the third wave. But, the rising tide is observable and necessary.

References

Atlanta Constitution Staff (1987) "Alas, Georgia Gets What It Pays For." *Atlanta Constitution* (20 March):22-A.

Brizius, Jack (1989) "Education Reform. We Owe It to the Kids." *The Entrepreneurial Economy Review* 7(5):3–8.

Corporation for Enterprise Development (1987) *Making the Grade: The Development Report Card for the States.* Washington, DC.

Corporation for Enterprise Development (1988) *Making the Grade: The 1988 Development Report Card for the States.* 2nd ed. Washington, DC.

Corporation for Enterprise Development (1989) *The 1989 Development Report Card for the States.* Washington, DC.

Denison, Edward F. (1985) *Trends in American Economic Growth, 1929–1982.* Washington, DC: The Brookings Institution.

Friedman, Robert E. (1987) "Flexible Manufacturing Networks." *The Entrepreneurial Economy* 6(1):2-4.

Friedman, Robert E. (1988) *The Safety Net as Ladder: Transfer Payments and Economic Development.* Washington, DC: Council of State Policy and Planning Agencies.

Hansen, Derek "Pete" (1988). "Entrepreneurship and the Culture of Development Finance." *The Entrepreneurial Economy Review* 7(3):3–5.

Hatch, C. Richard (1987) "Learning from Italy's Industrial Renaissance." *The Entrepreneurial Economuy* 6 (1):4–10.

Hudson Institute (1987) *Workforce 2000 Report.* Washington, DC: U.S. Department of Labor.

Plastrik, Peter and Steve Rohde (1988). "The Michigan Strategic Fund: Roots and Results." *The Entrepreneurial Economy Review* 7(3):6–15.

COMMENTS

John Rees

The chapter by Robert Friedman on "Job Creation, Business Growth, and State Policy: Glimpses of the Third Wave" presents us with considerable food for thought. While I find myself in agreement with much of Friedman's remarks, I want to comment on two areas in particular: one dealing with the context from which the chapter comes and the other dealing with what I perceive to be one of its more important concepts, the way that states have tried to encourage the development of entrepreneurs recently. Strategies for enhancing the development of entrepreneurial activities have not been given appropriate attention in state economic development policies until the 1980s.

The Development Report Card for the States initiated by the Corporation for Enterprise Development is based on four indicators of a state's economic health: economic performance, business vitality, business capacity, and state development policy. The origin of the Report Card lies in the corporation's considerable dissatisfaction with the methodology used in the Grant Thornton annual survey of manufacturing climates in the 48 contiguous states.

> The Grant Thornton index does not measure the factors important to business success in today's economy. The index, and the traditional business climate definition it perpetuates, are relics from another time, another economy. (Corporation for Enterprise Development, 1987, p. 2)

While I sympathize with the previous statement, this does not mean that the methodology used in the Report Card is not open to criticism. I do not intend to dwell on such criticisms here for they have been adequately covered elsewhere (Skoro, 1988). But one of Skoro's statements is worth repeating here:

> Grant Thornton, which is essentially the result of a poll of lobbyists for manufacturers, and *Making the Grade*, which is essentially a reply to that poll, should be labeled and recognized for what they are—political statements that have little verifiable economic content. (p. 152)

While one could debate the severity of the above statement, the Corporation for Enterprise Development does at least recognize the kind of political deter-

125

minism behind its indices. The essential point here is that "business climate" is a difficult concept to measure because it means different things to different people. To date, the brave efforts of Robert Friedman and the Corporation for Enterprise Development are among the best available for state policy makers to use, with an appropriate dose of caution.

The total amount of state investment in the new programs in all 50 states combined has been estimated at under $500 thousand for Fiscal Year 1988, which hardly qualifies for the title of "real money" in federal terms. Let's recall that during the last fiscal year the total dollar value of all state budgets combined came in under that for the federal deficit alone in Fiscal Year 1988. Because the 1980s has been a decade of experimentation for the states in the area of economic development, one of the ground rules of any experiment is the ability to fail and to fail again. I would remind Friedman that *accountability in this context may stifle creativity*.

When I suggest to Friedman and to state policy makers in general to be careful in their evaluation, this does not imply that we should not monitor developing situations over time. A recent study that I completed for the Economic Development Administration was an attempt to examine the experience of industry with the oldest of the new state programs, state-funded technology research centers, also known as "centers for excellence" or advanced technology centers (Rees, 1989). While I was skeptical about signs of success at the outset, my optimism increased as the results of the project emerged. I highlight a few results here:

1. Increased university-industry relationships in this country was not found to be a research enhancing strategy per se. Industry is getting more involved with universities out of its concern with its future labor force needs, a form of human capital or human resources strategy. We found that access to students and to faculty was the most important reason why industry gets involved with universities.

2. Companies saw no incentives in either the federal or state tax structures to engage in collaborative research with universities. Universities and government agencies were seen as relatively unimportant sources of technical knowledge by most companies. But when companies get involved with university technology centers, additional research was stimulated within 63 percent of participating companies. Furthermore, participation in center activities led to improvements in the quality of products and production methods in two-thirds of the companies that got involved.

3. We also found that states perceived as having the best track record for high technology development, like California and Massachusetts, were also seen as having the most effective state technology development programs, even though other states such as Pennsylvania, Ohio, New York, and Michigan have more comprehensive technology development programs to date.

What such a study shows is that we need to know much more about the impact of the new state programs on the industrial users. Creativity and long-run economic growth may be stifled if short-term political evaluations only take account of such superficial surrogates as the number of jobs created or matching funds obtained.

Again, it's these kinds of data behind the data that need to be examined if Friedman's Report Card is to continue to be useful to economic development officials and state policy makers.

References

Bhave, Mahesh Prabhakar (1988) "Entrepreneurial Firm Creation: Mapping the Process." Ph.D. dissertation, Syracuse University.

Corporation for Enterprise Development (1987) *Making the Grade: The Development Report Card for the States*, Washington, DC.

Hebert, Robert F. and Albert N. Link (1989) "In Search of the Meaning of Entrepreneurship." *Small Business Economics*, 1:39–49.

Rees, John (1989) *Industry Experience with Technology Research Centers, Final Report*, U.S. Department of Commerce, Economic Development Administration, Technical Assistance and Research Division.

Rees, John. and Robert Bradley (1988). "State Science Policy and Economic Development in the United States: A Critical Perspective." *Environment and Planning* 20:999–1012.

Skoro, Charles L. (1988) "Rankings of State Business Climates: An Evaluation of Their Usefulness in Forecasting." *Economic Development Quarterly* 2:138–52.

INDEX